D0627986

Toward a Renewal
of Sacramental Theology

Raymond Vaillancourt

Translated by Matthew J. O'Connell

 THE LITURGICAL PRESS
Collegeville, Minnesota

NIHIL OBSTAT: Joseph C. Kremer, S.T.L., *Censor Deputatus.*
IMPRIMATUR: ✠George H. Speltz, D.D., Bishop of St. Cloud.
March 13, 1979.

Toward a Renewal of Sacramental Theology is the authorized English translation of *Vers un Renouveau de la Théologie Sacramentaire* by Raymond Vaillancourt, copyright © 1977 by La Corporation des Editions Fides, Montreal.
Printed in the United States of America.

Cover design by Monica Bokinskie.

10	9	8	7	6	5	4

Library of Congress Cataloging in Publication Data
Vaillancourt, Raymond.
    Toward a renewal of sacramental theology.
    Translation of Vers un renouveau de la théologie sacramentaire.
    Bibliography: p.
    No. 1 Sacraments—Catholic Church.
    I. Title.
B.X.2200.V3413
      234'.16   79—12621
ISBN 0-8146-1050-1

Contents

Preface

The pastoral ministry of the sacraments is at present going through a difficult period, and for many the crisis comes as an unexpected disillusionment. They had thought that the conciliar reform with its subsequent revision of the liturgical books and updating of the rituals would give a new impetus to the liturgical movement and inaugurate a time of sure and continuous progress. The first years after the Council strengthened this impression, since the introduction of the first changes met with widespread approval among Christians—at least among those Christians who continued to take part in liturgical gatherings. But it became clear with time—and the fact was painful to acknowledge—that all these efforts at renewal were not checking the rapid decline in "practice." Now we find ourselves faced with the new and disturbing situation created by the increasing numbers of people who, when occasion offers, request the sacraments of a Church from which they have to some extent separated themselves. In these cases, what meaning do the sacraments have, either for these people who hold themselves aloof or for the Church that celebrates with them?

It was in this context that the question of meaning was initially raised. But the perspective quickly broadened, and we now see that the question is of concern to every Christian and to the Church itself. Why the sacraments? Why does the Church need these symbolic actions to express its faith and its relationship to God? What is the significance of this sacramental activity? What "power" does it contain? The need for a new way of talking about the sacraments is felt on all sides. It is no longer enough to repeat the language of a former age; instead it has become indispensable to invent once again a language that is intelligible to our contemporaries, a language that cannot be accused of reflecting a magical mentality but will nonetheless express the dynamism of the sacraments in all its fullness, without any watering down. This is a task that can no longer be avoided.

Seen from this point of view, the present crisis is beneficial in that it raises basic questions of meaning and induces us to pursue the aggiornamento in greater depth. In any future pastoral ministry of the sacraments, we cannot be content with the "how," but must push on to the "why."

This is the road the members of the Interdiocesan Commission for Liturgy of the Montreal region found themselves traveling as they undertook to study the pastoral approach to the sacraments of Christian initiation. At the outset we were admittedly more preoccupied with concrete ways and means, but we were gradually forced to face questions of meaning. At this point in our work we made an appeal for the collaboration of theologians, and as a result Fr. Raymond Vaillancourt joined our group. His participation stimulated and gave a new impetus to our exchanges, which went on over a period of several months and were both interesting and profitable. For this we are very grateful to him.

Today I have two reasons for rejoicing at the publication of Father Vaillancourt's book. First of all, I will find in it, in a more developed form, the substance of what he told us. Secondly, I am hereby assured that others in turn will profit from this synthesis. If the pastoral ministry of the sacraments is to receive a new impetus, all those in charge of it—pastors, members of pastoral teams for baptism and marriage, those in charge of confirmation, instructors in religion, and so on—must reflect together along these lines. Such thinking will, in my view, be all the more fruitful if it is done in teams and with constant reference to concrete experience and to the questions raised by Christian communities. Father Vaillancourt's book will be a stimulating guide for such groups, for it is based on a positive anthropology and offers in clear language a coherent and dynamic vision of the sacraments.

Only through a concerted effort at a thorough grasp of meaning and a renewal of theological language will Christian communities be able to go on being, in their celebration of the sacraments, a proclamatory sign to the world of God's salvation.

Clément Farly

Introduction

The renewal inaugurated by the Second Vatican Council has occasioned a great deal of reflection and study in the Church, a new awareness of situations, and pastoral analyses and choices that have made their effects felt in a number of areas and especially in the area of the sacramental expression of Christian experience. In relation to the universal Church, the renewal has found expression first in the Constitution on the Liturgy[1] and then in the revision of all the sacramental rituals. The national and local Churches and the Christian communities, for their part, have devoted a good deal of energy to pastoral reflection on the sacraments. Those active in the pastoral ministry have analyzed the situation in the Christian communities; this has led to an awareness of some painful facts, but also to much thoughtful scrutiny and eventually to various pastoral options of a prudential kind.

Now that a decade has passed since the beginning of this renewal, it is time to attempt a theological reading of this great movement for the revitalization of sacramental life. The aim of the present work, therefore, is to draw up a first balance sheet for the ongoing liturgical renewal and to put some questions to sacramental theology in order to find out to what extent it can shed light on, challenge, and direct the manner in which present-day Christian communities are expressing themselves in the sacraments.

The liturgical renewal seems to be raising some serious questions for classical sacramental theology. It can even be said that

---

1. The conciliar Constitution *Sacrosanctum Concilium* (December 4, 1963).

the renewal is proceeding without reference to this theology. As a result, it is undermining the coherence which this sacramental theology had acquired since the Middle Ages, so much so that the theology with which we are familiar is no longer an instrument capable of criticizing, analyzing, and directing the pastoral ministry of the sacraments and the sacramental life itself. How is it possible to make any use of the classical theses on validity and liceity, causality, and the matter and form of the sacraments in connection with the reformed sacramental liturgy? For practical purposes, we find ourselves here in two different worlds. The theology of the sacraments must therefore be revised. It is the task of the contemporary theologian to offer a new sacramental theology that will, on the one hand, be once again consistent with the other major theological disciplines, such as ecclesiology, Christology, and anthropology, and that will, on the other hand, be capable of preserving the elements of the ecclesial heritage.

The present reflections are addressed especially to pastors and the many pastoral workers who are engaged in the sacramental ministry. The purpose is not to supply new pastoral ways of doing things, although our reflections will repeatedly refer to concrete cases. The theologian's task is not to take the pastor's place but to provide him with a grill for theological reflection. This is why the aim of this book is first and foremost to offer a theological instrument that will help in evaluating the sacramental life and the movement of renewal that is accompanying it. It is a matter of helping pastoral ministers to evaluate the sacramental life of the community, to challenge and criticize the kind of pastoral approach they are taking in this area, to understand better the renewal of the liturgy, and to grasp its major orientations so as to profit fully by them and thus better fulfill the Church's vocation in regard to the sacraments.

The plan of this book is at once simple and ambitious. It is simple in its logic and clarity; it is ambitious in the questions it raises and especially in the challenges it seeks to issue. In the first part, we shall try to draw up a short balance sheet of the liturgical renewal and the pastoral ministry of the sacraments, both in terms of values and limitations and in terms of the questions this renewal and ministry raise for the theology of the sacraments.

In the second part, it will be important to see how the renewal of ecclesiology, Christology, and anthropology, all three of them essential components of the sacramental order, is a challenge to classical sacramental theology and at the same time supplies the basis for a theology of the sacraments that is new in its approaches and content as well as in its vocabulary.

The third part is more ambitious and offers a new essay at a sacramental theology. The essay endeavors to retain the riches of the ecclesial heritage while at the same time profiting by the new approaches in Christology, ecclesiology, and anthropology, and using the theological terminology established by the conciliar renewal.

The Liturgical Renewal and Some Questions for Sacramental Theology

There is no denying that the sacramental renewal inaugurated by the Second Vatican Council has stirred a great deal of enthusiasm among the Christian people. This is because of the basic Christian values that the Council has accentuated. At the same time, however, the enthusiasm frequently runs into major obstacles that dampen vital impulses and limit ambitions for the renewal which the contemporary liturgical movement is advocating. What are these values that evoke such an energetic response from those engaged in pastoral activity? How, on the other hand, can we identify the limiting forces that put a brake on the efforts at renewal? How may we relate this period of the Church's life to the sacramental theology and sacramental life of past centuries? What questions does the renewal raise for classical sacramental theology? Finally, what is the task of today's theologians? This chapter seeks to give an answer to these basic questions, together with a number of others, as it relates the liturgical renewal to classical sacramental theology.

1 — The Values Promoted by the Liturgical Renewal

It is rather obvious that certain undeniable values are being promoted by the liturgical renewal as this finds expression in the revision of the sacramental rites, in the norms for celebrating these rites, and in pastoral practice relating to the sacramental life. There is satisfaction, by and large, with the basic direction of the new rituals and with the opportunities given to the Christian people to facilitate their conscious, intelligent, and free participation in liturgical actions. There is approval likewise of the many possibilities for introducing Christians to a new dimension of meaning in connection with one or other specific life situation. Generally speaking, it must be acknowledged that in its program of renewal the Council has succeeded in turning the great values and tendencies of contemporary man into a basis for the sacramental expression of Christian faith. More specifically, the values in question can be subsumed under the following headings: authenticity of expression and connection with human life; participation and communion; creativity and spontaneity; importance of the word of God; importance of meaning.

Authenticity of expression and connection with life

The desire for self-expression is not only one of the claims most frequently made by our contemporaries; it also represents one of the human being's most basic needs. This is because the human being attains to fulfillment through self-expression. This is a truth well known to people who have felt themselves unable to develop in a given milieu, whether it be that of the family or the community or some other. When the opportunity came, they found a new milieu in which to live and work, and in a relatively short time they were changed people. They began to blossom, to be productive and inventive and quite sure of themselves. What happened? The new environment in which they were now living enabled them to give expression to their potentialities and through this self-expression to bring their being and personality to fulfillment.

The conciliar renewal discerned this need. The entire renewal of the liturgy and of the rituals relates to this need for true and authentic self-expression. The Christian liturgy thus becomes a locus of vital self-expression. As a result there is a close connection between sacramental expression and the life both of the people of God generally and of each participant in particular.

The Constitution on the Liturgy sets forth the principles behind this expression and this connection with life. The rituals clearly show a concern to meet the vital needs of people, to link up with their daily experience, and to foster the authentic expression of their lives in their entirety, within the perspective of faith.

Participation and communion

In order to promote the self-expression of the person and the connection of the liturgy with the concrete lives of people, the sacramental renewal has given a privileged place to various means of participation and communion. I am speaking of such things as

2

the use of the vernaculars, the possibility of adaptation and choice in prayers, biblical texts, and so on. Vital self-expression within the perspectives of faith requires participation and community. Genuine communion is incompatible with anonymity. It is interesting to note that the emphasis on communion in the liturgical renewal of Vatican II corresponds to a desire and need for communion and brotherhood that has grown in direct proportion to the ever-increasing anonymity of our large cities.

The renewal has pointed out quite specific means of effecting communion and participation. First, there is the use of the vernacular.[1] In addition, Vatican II opened the door for adaptation and choice in regard to prayers and texts. This freedom is anything but unrealistic, since it enables pastors to develop a liturgy which "sticks close to real life" or, in other words, appeals to what is deepest and most vital in the Christian. In this way his very life can become a locus of revelation and celebration.

Creativity and spontaneity

Moving on from the desire for an authentic expression of faith and the desire for participation and communion, the revision of the rituals has also put the stamp of approval, as it were, on a quite new tendency: the tendency to creativity and spontaneity. It can legitimately be called "quite new," because it represents a break with a tradition, several centuries old, of ritualism. We might say that Vatican II has, paradoxically, replaced the rubric of ritualism with the rubric of spontaneity and creativity.

This new departure suggests two remarks. The first is that creativity and spontaneity are not a call for amateurism and slovenliness. The liturgy continues to be governed by theological, psychological, and pastoral norms that are not to be scorned. On the other hand, since the sacramental expression of the faith cannot be the product of speculative thought alone, it is important to use the resources life itself provides. Life, however, cannot be comprehended once and for all, but is perceived differently depending on situations. Here is where spontaneity and creativity have their place. "Spontaneity" and "creativity" may be taken as referring to the use of living symbols that are perceived as natural and do not require learned explanations to be understood by the human mind and heart. Spitting at and cursing evil spirits cannot have the same meaning in our day that they once had.

---

1. Constitution on the Liturgy, no. 36.

Spontaneity means that no symbol must be forced on anyone and that certain symbols can even be rejected if they do not correspond to the conception of the world that is generally accepted in this or that region of the world, or if they do not fit in with the life of the community. This amounts to saying that spontaneity requires far more than permission to use alternate ways of carrying out a rite. It implies, above all, an accord between the symbol and those who make use of it in order to express the inexpressible. In this regard, the line adopted by the Second Vatican Council reaches back to the practice of the early Christian liturgies, since for the latter the rubrics were simply suggestions, inspirations, incentives, starting points, models and examples.[2]

The second remark has to do with the evident discrepancy between the openness of Vatican II and the norms issued by the Congregation for the Sacraments and Divine Worship for applying the conciliar principles, and the warnings that accompany them. If we read carefully the Constitution on the Liturgy, we cannot but be surprised at the openness to adaptation and creativity. The principles are clearly stated.

On the other hand, as the new rituals, which on the whole apply in a fairly broad manner the principles enunciated in the Constitution, are put into use, those in charge seem to be closing the door to creativity. Warnings are issued on every side to prevent abuses, to such an extent that some believe they can detect a closing of minds at the level of the application of principles. What is happening? It seems necessary to stand back a bit if we are to appreciate what is going on. On the one hand, Vatican II stated a number of principles that foster creativity. On the other hand, these principles cannot be applied overnight. The Congregation for the Sacraments and Divine Worship is concerned that the application be gradual and that people be properly formed for this new kind of liturgy. We should regard the restrictions, therefore, as a prudential measure and not as a rejection of the conciliar principles. And in a number of cases there is a good reason for the restriction. For the fact that a priest has been celebrating the Eucharist regularly for years does not automatically make him capable of composing a Eucharistic prayer.

Those who preside at celebrations of the sacraments need a special competence if they are to supply the liturgical action with modern words and symbols and not either betray it or narrow its

---

2. This was the nature of the first rituals which Hippolytus of Rome provided and which are now to be found in the collection known as the *Apostolic Tradition*.

scope.[3] In short, then, we should interpret these apparent restrictions as pedagogical measures intended to channel desires and inspirations, and not as a form of resistance to the current of creativity set free by Vatican II.

Importance of the word of God

The general norms of the Constitution on the Liturgy give a great deal of importance to the word of God. We shall cite articles 24 and 35.

Sacred scripture is of the greatest importance in the celebration of the liturgy. For it is from it that lessons are read and explained in the homily, and psalms are sung. It is from the scriptures that the prayers, collects, and hymns draw their inspiration and their force, and that actions and signs derive their meaning. Hence in order to achieve the restoration, progress, and adaptation of the sacred liturgy it is essential to promote that sweet and living love for sacred scripture to which the venerable tradition of Eastern and Western rites gives testimony (no. 24; Flannery, p. 10).

That the intimate connection between rites and words may be apparent in the liturgy:

(1) In sacred celebrations a more ample, more varied, and more suitable reading from sacred scripture should be restored.

(2) The most suitable place for a sermon ought to be indicated in the rubrics, for a sermon is part of the liturgical action whenever a rite involves one. The ministry of preaching is to be fulfilled most faithfully and carefully. The sermon, moreover, should draw its content mainly from scriptural and liturgical sources, for it is the proclamation of God's wonderful works in the history of salvation, which is the mystery of Christ ever made present and active in us, especially in the celebration of the liturgy.

(3) Instruction which is more explicitly liturgical should also be given in a variety of ways. If necessary, short directives to be spoken by the priest or competent minister should be provided within the rites themselves. But they should be given only at suitable moments and in prescribed words or their equivalents (no. 35; Flannery, pp. 12–13).

These two passages from the conciliar Constitution indicate the place of the word of God in the liturgy of the sacraments. Article 24 states the great importance of the word of God in liturgical celebrations, while article 35 specifies some places and times for reading this word during the celebration. In order that the word may carry its full weight of meaning, place is made for directives and commentaries even during the celebration.

---

3. On this subject see La Maison-Dieu, no. 111 (1972): "Créativité et liturgie."

The new rituals seem to have done a good job of illustrating and implementing the principle that the word of God is to be given a privileged place in the celebration. All the rituals include a liturgy of the word; even the ritual of private reconciliation suggests a form, brief indeed but nonetheless real, of liturgy of the word. Within these liturgies of the word, a number of new arrangements, a choice of readings from Scripture, a choice of themes, songs, psalms, prayers, and so on, help to highlight the word of God and to make it yield the maximum of meaning called for by the situation in which those who celebrate a particular event live their lives.

This great effort at restoring the liturgy by giving the word of God its proper place is in continuity with primitive tradition. It also gives an answer to the questions the reformers addressed to the liturgy of their day. In addition, it seeks to bring out as fully as possible the meaning of the event in human experience; this is another value cultivated in this effort at renewal.

The importance of meaning

There is another point to which we must draw attention as being one of the values highlighted in the renewal of the sacramental liturgy, namely, the importance assigned to meaning. The entire renewal, both that which is advocated in the Constitution on the Liturgy and that which has been inaugurated by the new rituals, locates sacramental life within a definite universe of meaning. It thus renders the Christian people less susceptible to the temptation of giving the sacramental rites a magical interpretation. The texts of the Constitution and the rituals manifest a real concern that every gesture, every word, every text should touch the community and the individuals who make it up at the level of their deepest experience during the celebration. No one wants any more celebrations that lend themselves to a magical interpretation. All want meaningful celebrations that can evoke a maximum of significance from the actual experience of people and, on the basis of this experience, reveal to them what they themselves are, what they are called to be, and what God is for them.

This understanding of the importance of meaning lies behind the concern for the adaptation of the new rituals to the various cultures, social classes, generations, and so on. It shows in the opportunity given Christians of constructing, as it were, their own celebration by choosing the themes, readings from Scripture, prayers, songs, and so forth. It also shows in each and every major part of the rituals.

Take, for example, the ceremony of welcome in the liturgy of a sacrament. This ceremony is meaningful not only psychologically but theologically as well. When done in a suitable way, the ceremony of welcome undoubtedly creates an atmosphere of openness and sympathy while also situating those present in a context of prayer and faith. This is a first benefit that is located primarily at the psychological level. But the ceremony of welcome also has another benefit that may be termed theological. The ceremony not only creates a climate and context of faith but is also intended to give concrete expression to the welcome God extends to a person or community.

When an infant is baptized, for example, the ceremony of welcome is not just a matter of the priest greeting the people at the back of the church. No, the entire community present, along with the child's father and mother, is welcoming a new life. It is the community that comes to meet a new human being, and it does so in the name of God who welcomes this new being into existence, promises it his help, and invites it to grow and reach fulfillment. In a sense it is God, in the persons of the assembled community, who extends his arms to this little human being that is now beginning its life. The community gives a concrete visible form to the welcome God is extending to the newcomer. In the light of our faith we say that God does the welcoming, but he does it concretely through the agency of the father, the mother, and their kinsfolk. Thus it can be said that the entire family plays a theological role in welcoming a new life.

In this context, the role of the priest is very important; it goes beyond sprinkling holy water and shaking hands. It is for him to make the community present become aware of the theological significance of his action and his joy as well as of their own role on the occasion of the birth of a child into a family. He must make them realize that the welcome they now celebrate is a sign of the welcome they must extend to the child throughout its life in order that it may be able to attain to its fulfillment.

2 — The Limitations of the Renewal

It would be self-deception to believe that the values or ideals which inspired the liturgical renewal of Vatican II have been put fully into practice. On the contrary, there is a significant gap between these theoretical ideals and their concrete implementation. What is the source of these limitations? It appears to be twofold: one is inherent in the rituals, the other is external and consists in the mentality of pastors and faithful.

The ambiguity of the rituals

Despite the new directions taken by the rituals, it is clear that they reflect at times two mentalities, two theologies, and that as a result the very change which the rituals advocate is hindered. The new ritual of reconciliation provides examples of this kind of intrinsic theological ambiguity. On the one hand, the ritual is one of those that most clearly bear the stamp of new theological approaches to man, the Church, salvation, and sin. On the other hand, it also reflects certain approaches to sin that are overly individualistic. It also requires that the various kinds of celebration fulfill identical functions, when in fact they are meant to fulfill very different ones. Thus to expect of a communal celebration what is proper to a private celebration, and vice versa, is to fail to follow the logic of the theological choice which provided the starting point. It is therefore to risk preventing a new form for the celebration of reconciliation from taking root.

Here we have a limitation that is internal to the very documents on which the renewal is based. There are many others that come from outside the rituals, either from pastors and others active in the pastoral ministry or from Christians who are emerging from a period in which the context was quite different.

Mentality of pastors and Christian people

By and large, pastors are happy with the directions taken in the new rituals and with the possibilities offered to the Christian people for conscious, intelligent, and free participation in the liturgical actions. They are happy, too, to have the opportunity of introducing Christians to a new realm of meaning on the occasion of some specific situation in their lives.

On the other hand, it is proving very difficult for pastors to apply the directives provided by the renewal. This is to be expected, since pastors of a certain age think and act in ways that reflect a quite different spirit. Thus it is difficult, if not impossible, for them to be presidents and celebrants when all they have learned is how to be "officiants" performing a rite. Nor should we believe that only pastors of a certain age group are setting limits to the renewal sought by Vatican II. The renewal will continue to demand a great deal of those presiding at celebrations, and we must not be surprised to see even pastors whose formation has been more recent experiencing the same difficulties as their elders. The new liturgy as a whole represents a novel challenge to everyone who is to preside at, guide, and be responsible for the liturgy.

In addition to the special problem of their formation, those who preside at the liturgy share with the Christian people a mentality which likewise limits the renewal initiated by Vatican II. First of all, the people of Western Christendom as a whole are emerging from a lengthy period of immobilism and ritualism that might be called the "age of the minimum." In that past time Christians were undoubtedly honoring God and "receiving the sacraments." But their form of worship, characterized as it was by uniformity and ritualism, too often caused them to be content with the minimum required for the valid celebration of what the Lord wanted. For example, the validity of a Mass celebrated with a congregation of five hundred people required that only the celebrant communicate. We recognize in this description the Sunday Masses of twenty-five years ago, at which indeed the priest alone received Communion. Or recall how baptism was celebrated: usually in the sacristy and with only the priest, the father, and the sponsors present.

This mentality gave the Christian people a restricted vision of what a sacrament is. In the perspective thus created, the distinction between validity and liceity, and its importance, played a prominent role, as did the theses on matter and form which, though very rich in their basic intuition, trained Christians in the rule of the minimum. This restrictive vision is something that still needs to be eliminated.

The immobilism that characterized the sacramental life in recent centuries and was diffused by means of a fussy ritualism has likewise left its mark on the Christian people. This trait is not the least of the obstacles to a renewal of sacramental life. Those active in the pastoral ministry who take the directives of the renewal as their inspiration must not only invent the concrete details of a renewed liturgy; they are often forced also to justify the least change! What an effort this requires of someone who sees clearly the real state of sacramental life today! On the other hand, the reaction of many Christians is only to be expected; it is but the fruit of the education given for several centuries now.

Part of the inherited mentality is what might be called a "pinpointing" conception of a sacrament, which is betrayed in such questions as these: "What precise change does confirmation make in a child's life? What does confirmation give that baptism has

9

not already given?" This view identifies the sacrament with the rite and with a specific moment, namely, the moment of the celebration. It is difficult, therefore, for pastors to conceive of the celebration of a sacrament as being extended in time, and for many of the faithful to accept the idea of a sacrament as an ongoing reality. The rite is so important in their eyes that they have little interest in what precedes and follows it.

In addition, a very individualistic conception of the sacramental life, according to which salvation is identified with a personal gift of God to each believer at a certain moment in his or her life, is preventing the sacramental renewal from sinking deeper roots, for the renewal emphasizes the community and inverts certain perspectives. This is strikingly clear when it comes to the communal celebration of reconciliation. To understand properly this kind of celebration, people must put aside an individualistic approach and become aware that something quite different is going on.

The individualistic conception of the sacraments is connected with another that might be called the "anthropocentric conception of the sacraments." Under the influence of this view, the Christian focuses exclusively on himself, on his own commitment, and on the change that takes place in him. Finally, the mentality of the Christian people is comparable to the magical outlook of pagan peoples. For even after centuries of Christianity, we are far from having christianized the religious mind of man at any profound level.

Separation of sacramental liturgy from life

We have seen that one emphasis in the liturgical renewal is on the link between liturgy and life. Pastors are endeavoring to make the link a real one, but their efforts are being hindered by a centuries-long separation of liturgy from life. The separation makes its presence known through the various paraliturgies that have developed since the Middle Ages. We may think, for example, of Benediction of the Blessed Sacrament, the multitudinous devotions, the Forty Hours, and so on. These paraliturgies were really attempts to make up for a liturgy that was no longer connected with real life and was marked by ritualism, immobilism, and so forth. The paraliturgies were assuming the role that the sacramental liturgy should have been exercising.

Thus, despite the efforts of pastors to turn the sacramental liturgy into a celebration that is in close contact with life, some people still retain a fixist view of the sacraments and continue to think of the liturgy as so grand and mysterious that they are content not to understand it or to relate it in faith to their real-life situation. Others are nostalgic for the devotions and para-liturgies that played in their lives the real and effective role which the liturgy has not yet succeeded fully in regaining.

3 — The Historical Context of the Renewal

It is of interest to observe that the present renewal of sacramental theology and sacramental life is not the first such in the history of the Church. It seems of some importance to situate our own period in its historical context if we are to understand the present time of renewal by comparison with the past and with the goal to which the Church's sacramental life is now being oriented. We have good reason, it seems, for saying that the Church is entering upon a new phase as far as the sacramental expression of faith is concerned. She has already passed through two great phases. The first comprised her experience of the sacraments from the first Christian communities down to those of the Middle Ages. The Middle Ages then began the development of a technical concept of the sacraments that produced a new type of sacramental theology and sacramental life; this was the second phase and has been coextensive with the Church's life down to our own day.

In the present liturgical renewal, the Church is taking a different approach to the way it should pursue its calling in regard to the sacraments. Beyond a doubt, this new approach is introducing us to a third phase in the history of the Church's sacramental life.

In order to better understand the contemporary period, we shall briefly describe the preceding phases and bring out their major orientations. Then it will be easier for us to see in what respect the postconciliar period represents innovation and is turning away from what has been familiar to us until now.

First period: From sacramentality to sacramental rite

During the first period, which comprises the first millennium, the Church became progressively conscious of its calling with regard to the sacramental life, but it did not attain to any very precise concept of the sacramental phenomenon as such. The first Christian communities sought to experience more fully the major events that occurred in the midst of ordinary life by relating them to the paschal mystery of Christ. They gradually discovered that a number of human situations could be privileged occasions

11

for proclaiming and revealing to all, Christian or non-Christian, the profound meaning of certain events in human life.

The New Testament narratives are very reserved when it comes to speaking about the sacramental experience of the first Christian communities. Except for the Lord's Supper and baptism, the other sacramental rites which have been clearly identified since the Middle Ages can make but little reference to Christian experience as described by the New Testament writers.

At the Lord's Supper (see 1 Cor. 11:17-33; Mt. 26:26-29), the first Christians were aware of reliving the paschal mystery of Christ and entering into the saving work he had accomplished. Similarly, baptism actualized, or made present and operative, the death and resurrection of Christ in each person who accepted Christ's plan for him or her as presented by the community.

We know practically nothing of the liturgical or cultic contours of these two actions in the first Christian communities. We are, however, given precise information about the meaning of the two rites, or what might be called their theological contours. The aim of these rites was to establish a relationship between the person's present life and the paschal mystery of Christ. A relation seems to have been discerned between Christian worship and the events of the historical life of Jesus. Cullmann goes even further and says that the Gospel of John "seeks to point to the full identity of the Lord, present in the early Christian congregation, with the historical Jesus."[4]

Continuing Jewish tradition as it does, the Lord's Supper is a memorial. It commemorates the central event of salvation: the death and resurrection of Christ which had been prefigured in the old covenant; it shows that salvation is effectively present now in and through the daily lives of men; and it prefigures an even fuller salvation which man is called to obtain in the eschatological kingdom.[5] In order that they might enter in a more meaningful way into this mystery of salvation, the participants were required to be attuned to the requirements of the revealed mystery. In the Jewish liturgy, the Passover meal was intended to place the participants in an exodus situation; thus they were bidden to repeat the actions of their ancestors, namely, to eat the lamb

---

4. *Early Christian Worship*, tr. A. S. Todd and J. B. Torrance (Studies in Biblical Theology 10; Naperville, Ill., 1953), pp. 37–38.
5. St. Thomas adopts this thesis on the memorial character of the Jewish liturgy in his explanation of the three dimensions of a sacramental sign; see *Summa theologiae* III, q. 60, a. 3.

with "your loins girded, your sandals on your feet, and your staff in your hand."[6] In a similar perspective, St. Paul exhorts the inhabitants of Corinth to make themselves worthy of the mysteries they celebrate.[7]

The same pattern holds for baptism. In Paul's view, baptism is related to the event of Christ's death and resurrection.[8] It also signifies a death and resurrection in the course of man's present life as well as his death at the end and his subsequent resurrection in the eschatological kingdom. The New Testament accounts of baptism do not have many cultic resonances, although baptism did very soon acquire a liturgical context for Christians. But the liturgical dimension was not the important one. The emphasis was chiefly on participation in the salvation won by the death and resurrection of Christ. "Participating" meant accepting the message or becoming conscious of the mystery revealed by Jesus and adhering to it. "Baptism" seems in fact to be synonymous with "being converted," "believing," "being cleansed," "being sanctified," "being justified."

Even if the Christian communities had not yet reached a very precise notion of a sacrament in their theological reflection, it is clear that they lived an intense liturgical life. Think, for example, of the signs developed for Christian initiation in the first centuries and of the extensive elaboration of these in the patristic period.

As for the other sacramental signs which have been accepted as such since the Middle Ages, they have a long history in which the Church can be seen becoming progressively more aware of its vocation in regard to the sacramental life. In one sense, the Christian communities might well have rested content with the signs of Christian initiation. These contained everything; all the dimensions of the paschal mystery were to be found in them. But the Church quickly became conscious that if it restricted itself to these signs it could not render fully explicit the many dimensions of the Christian mystery. The Church's vocation in regard to the sacramental life could not therefore be limited to the use of these few signs. At the same time, the Church also became aware that a number of human situations provided it with privileged occasions for exercising this vocation. Let us look at a few instances.

---

6. Ex. 12:11.
7. 1 Cor. 11:17-33.
8. Rom. 6:1-11.

13

As far as the sacrament of reconciliation was concerned, the Church became conscious of it simply on the basis of its own experience. It can be said that this sacramental action came into existence as an ecclesial answer to a question that arose in the first Christian communities. Realizing as they did their role as sacrament of Christ in the pagan world of the day, the communities sought to present an image of perfection or holiness. As St. Paul says: "Christ loved the Church and gave himself up for her, having cleansed her by the washing of water with the word, that he might present the Church to himself in splendor, without spot or wrinkle or any such thing."[9] Christians should be holy.

But problems arise when a baptized Christian proves false to the ideal of holiness required by the very nature of the Church as sacrament of Christ. As early as the time of St. Paul, the question very soon presented itself at Corinth, for example, because of the undesirables who bore the name of "brothers" and yet were unchaste (1 Cor. 5:1-12). Sinners within the community are a danger to the Church: they are a leaven of corruption in the community at large (1 Cor. 5); they detract from the truthfulness of the Eucharistic celebration (1 Cor. 11:29-34); and they invalidate the testimony of the community because they make the life of the community a lie. To this problem, which affected the very existence of the community, an ecclesial answer had to be found, that is, an answer that operates on the same level as the problem itself. A passage in Matthew (18:15-18) tells us the answer the community was prompted to find.

Little by little, then, the community became aware of the need for a rite of ecclesial reconciliation. In doing so, the community revealed the face of God the reconciler to itself and to all who found themselves in a situation of conflict and sin. It was his sacrament that the community wanted to be in its daily life. At the same time, it revealed man's true situation as well as the ecclesial implications of his sinfulness. It is worth noting here that the point of departure for this sacramental rite is not the individual but the community. In relation to the latter and its active sacramental role, the entire sacramental practice of the early Christian communities becomes intelligible; this remains true down to the time when private confession made its appearance.

The history of the sacrament of marriage likewise has aspects that are of interest to us. In the early centuries of the Church, the

---

9. Eph. 5:25-27.

Christian rite of marriage was practically nonexistent. Christians who were entering into marriage celebrated this event according to the rites and customs of their milieu. Only gradually did the Church become aware that here was another occasion for it to exercise its vocation in regard to the sacramental life. At the beginning, that is, throughout the first three centuries, Christians contracted marriage in accordance with local custom. There was no question as yet of a Christian liturgy of marriage with a special Mass and blessing.

Quite soon, however, the Church began to see this situation in people's lives in a Christian perspective and tried to show baptized Christians entering upon marriage the Christian significance of their new state of life. In order to do this, the bishop was urged to betake himself to the place of the wedding, and there to show the new couple this Christian meaning and give them his blessing. Beginning in the fourth century, this sacramental rite was set within a liturgy that was to become increasingly important.[10] Customs were retained insofar as they were compatible with the Christian view or marriage, but the Church gave them a more profound meaning. It showed, at the very heart of the Christian couple's life, the face of the God who is love.

A similar development seems to have taken place with regard to the anointing of the sick. With a well-identified human situation as the starting point, the Church delved more deeply into the paschal mystery and brought to light a particular dimension of it. It is true that at different periods communities emphasized various aspects of the sacrament. Thus, at one time the stress was on the complete remission of sins (therefore on the aspect of reconciliation); at another time, on the affirmation of eschatological life and thus on the renewal of the choice made in baptism; and at still another time, on bodily healing. The Church sought to respond to its vocation regarding the sacramental life with the help of these various theologies that arose in the life of the Christian communities. Its aim was to proclaim the message of liberation and hope to Christians whose health was under attack. It wanted to show them a God who was calling them to eschatological life and giving a meaning to their illness and even to their death, if that came, by having them share in the eschatological hope.

---

10. For more details, see E. Schillebeeckx, *Marriage: Human Reality and Saving Mystery,* tr. N. D. Smith (New York, 1965), and Th. Rey-Mermet, *Ce que Dieu a uni* (Paris, 1974).

We might likewise consider other sacramental practices such as the rites of ordination or the ceremonies for the consecration of kings and for monastic and religious profession. Even if the latter do not satisfy the technical definition of a sacrament that was elaborated in the Middle Ages, it is nonetheless true that they have a certain sacramental value, since they bear the name of "sacramentals." They provided the Church with further occasions for carrying out its vocation as sacrament of Christ by enabling Christians to see and live the meaning contained in certain situations of life, certain Christian commitments, and so on.

The ecclesial perspective that marked the sacramental practice of the Church in the first three centuries did not prevent a strong emphasis on the anthropological dimension. As a result, the liturgy of that period had as one of its principal concerns to be in contact with the life of the people; this in turn fostered liturgical creativity. This anthropological approach to the sacramental life was a quite different thing from the individualistic approach that was to be characteristic of sacramental life during the second historical phase.

In the individualistic approach, the Church is no longer the principal agent in the sacramental action. It is simply the place where the action occurs, while the individual becomes the principal actor. In this perspective, the individual acquires importance at the expense of the community's role. The individual takes steps to obtain his salvation, to rid himself of guilt and receive God's forgiveness, to receive various graces. We shall return to this point in dealing with the second phase.

The anthropological approach, on the other hand, is not exclusive of an ecclesial perspective. On the contrary, it provides the foundation for this perspective. The Church proclaims a certain reality of faith by integrating it into a human situation. In short, it is man's situation that provides the Church with the occasion for bringing out this or that aspect of the mystery of Christ in relation to this or that aspect of the meaning of human life.

In the writings of the Fathers of the Church who describe its life during the early centuries, we find great importance being assigned to proclamation or revelation in the sacramental rite. Conscious of its vocation to be the sacrament of Christ, the Church wants to reveal to Christians the many aspects of the mystery of salvation. It does this by enabling them to see at each new stage of human life a new aspect of the face of God as well as the full meaning a person can derive from this or that situation of life.

We can therefore understand the importance attributed to the baptismal and mystagogical catecheses of the early centuries. These were not simply a form of preparation; they were a part of the Church's sacramental action that would have its climax in the celebration of the rite.

It is worth noting, moreover, that while the origins of our word "sacrament" are obscure, it does have a certain connection with the Greek *mysterion* of St. Paul, a term which for him means the plan of God revealed by and in his Son, the man Jesus. This one *mysterion* had been prefigured in the old covenant and was now experienced in Christian liturgical celebrations. In this second form Christians spoke of *mysteria* in the plural. In Latin ecclesiastical language, *sacramentum* was used for the mysteries as celebrated in Christian worship. But our word "sacrament" does not designate solely the liturgical rite as such. It refers to the rite, of course, but to the rite as revealing, making present, celebrating the work of salvation done by Jesus Christ. In other words, the important thing is not the rite as such, but the rite insofar as it reveals God's plan of salvation.

The neglect of this aspect of proclamation or revelation in the Church's sacramental life in later centuries was to elicit the reaction of the Reformers. The latter would rediscover this dimension but would not be able to articulate it fully with the ritual aspect. As a result there would be two conceptions of the Church's life: that of the reformed Church, which would be known as the "Church of the word," and that of the Roman Catholic Church, which would be known as the "Church of the sacraments."

In the first phase of Church history, the aspect of proclamation or revelation seems to have been properly emphasized. It was taken as self-evident in fact, since in and through the sacraments Christians were endeavoring to carry out the Church's vocation of being the sacrament of Christ. A sacramental rite was a fine opportunity to fulfill this mission.

In order to exercise its vocation in regard to the sacramental life and to celebrate ritually the great stages of the revelation of the Christian mystery, the Church drew on biblical tradition and the Jewish liturgy as well as on the cultures of the age. Thus the rituals for the sacraments were developed. But we must be sure to grasp the spirit of these rituals. They were used quite differently than rituals have been in recent centuries: they were regarded simply as helps, as models. The early rituals were never meant as imposing a single way of carrying out a Christian celebration.

They were simply at the service of the Church in its sacramental activity. Unfortunately, toward the latter half of the first millennium they would be interpreted as mandating one and only one way of celebrating a situation or stage of human life.

Despite the positive character of the first period of sacramental life as we have described it, with its primary emphasis on the sacramental nature of the Church itself, Christians were moving toward the systematization and therefore the ritualism that were to be the major characteristics of the second phase.

Second period: The sacramental rite

Beginning in the Middle Ages, the theologians worked out a technical concept of sacrament that initiated a new period for the Church in what concerns its manner of understanding and living its sacramental nature and vocation. This period fostered new emphases. Thus it gave priority to personal experience, with the consequences this entailed, such as the importance of the role of the individual, the absence of the ecclesial perspective (thus leaving little room for the initiative of God himself as given concrete form by the community), the impression that man earns his salvation, and so on. It also assigned great importance to the value and efficacy of the sacramental rite as such, so much so that we can describe this period as the age of the sacramental rite. This is not meant to imply that other values were denied; it is simply to say that many questions were approached from the viewpoint of the rite. This is the case with such questions as the institution of the sacraments, their validity, their efficacy, and so on. The rite itself attracted the main attention of pastors, theologians, and Christian people.

All this is not to say that this period left a legacy of little value. On the contrary, the sacramental theology which developed in the West and received its most complete formulation from St. Thomas Aquinas possesses great merits, the coherent unity of which can best be grasped when seen in the context of the Christian theology of the age.

These merits represent permanent acquisitions for theological thinking. We may call attention first of all to the systematic reflection on the major intuitions of St. Thomas. This reflection has clarified a number of points by introducing distinctions and nuances that have been and will continue to be a valuable aid to anyone considering the sacramental expression of the faith.

More particularly, we must call attention to three specific

points. The first is that by locating the sacraments in the order of signs, St. Thomas put an end to several centuries of uncertainty as to the nature of a sacrament.[11] This position of his is not a merely theoretical one, for it situates the entire sacramental phenomenon in the universe of meaning. St. Thomas was able to profit from this initial position in most of the other questions of sacramental theology. Thus, by fidelity to it he was able (this is our second specific point) to articulate properly signification and efficacy.[12] In his view, a sacrament signifies as it causes grace, or it causes grace according to its capacity for signifying. This is a connection that should not be neglected; we shall return to this point. Then there is this third specific merit: the elucidation of the three dimensions or references of the sacramental sign (something that is too often overlooked in contemporary pastoral practice).[13]

Without in any way playing down these merits, we must also say that the sacramental theology of the Middle Ages, including that of St. Thomas, shows certain limitations. We may call attention to four critical areas.

As we know, this period developed a theology of Christ as head, along with its theology of the sacraments. This was a valuable acquisition, but as Father Congar observes, "it fostered a rather exclusively christological point of view that was not adequately complemented by a theology of the Holy Spirit."[14]

The second criticism relates to the absence of any ecclesiology at that time.[15] The treatise on the sacraments (in St. Thomas) followed the treatise on Christ, but we see today that there was no connecting link between the two, and this lack left its mark at various points. Thus the theologian passes directly from Christ to the individual, without sufficient reference to the ecclesial context. The question of the minister of the sacraments is perhaps the one most affected by the absence of reference to the Church. The theology of ministry was developed in relation to Christ by using the notion of juridical power, but there would have been a very different vision of the minister's role if the Church had been integrated into the picture and more extensive use made of the

---

11. *Summa theologiae* III, q. 60.
12. *Ibid.*, q. 62.
13. *Ibid.*, q. 60, a. 3.
14. Yves Congar, *Un peuple messianique* (Cogitatio fidei 85; Paris, 1975), p. 54.
15. The first treatises on the Church were occasioned by the dispute over the relative powers of Church and State; for example, the *De regimine christiano* of James of Vierbo, reprinted in the collection *Études de théologie historique* (Paris, 1926).

rich concept of signification which was in general so intensively utilized in the Middle Ages.

A third criticism has to do with the scholastic theological method of the period. As is generally known, this method puts a premium on analysis, on the breakdown of questions into their component parts, on the distinction of different formal aspects, and on the need of definition and precision.[16] The period undoubtedly made very valuable contributions, but it ran the risk of straitjacketing, as it were, the realities of faith, which are very difficult to grasp, in a technical vocabulary. This is the case with the classical questions of the number of the sacraments and their causality, efficacy, and validity.

A final criticism concerns something that did not derive from the theologians but nonetheless exercised an influence not only on the sacramental life but on sacramental theology as well. I refer to the mentality of the Christian masses, who were much more at home with the experience of the sacred and the religious than with Christian experience and who attributed great importance to the sacramental rite as such. This opened the way to a magical interpretation of the sacraments and consequently to a physicalist or reifying conception of the realities of faith that are signified by the sacraments, for example, grace, merit, and sin.

In trying to isolate the major characteristics of the sacramental life during this second phase, we note how far removed we are from the first phase, in which, as we have seen, the emphasis was on the sacramental nature of the Church and on the life people concretely live.

The prevailing popular mentality, with its magical, not to say pagan, inclination, focused all attention in the sacramental rite on the individual at the expense of the ecclesial dimension. The sacramental rite thus became a rite for the individual. The widespread practice of private confession is one proof of this. The whole vocabulary employed at the popular level of ecclesial life rather clearly reflects this individualistic approach to the sacraments. People still speak of making *their* first Communion, receiving *their* confirmation, performing *their* Easter duty, and so on. In the logic of this mentality, the sacramental life of the second phase has assigned an important place to the activity of man. This becomes a point of departure and the point of arrival for the sacramental rite, with little place left for the initiative of God as given

---

16. Congar, *ibid.*

concrete form in the role of the community.

We may take penance as an example. A person experiences conflict and guilt, and therefore takes steps to regain security and peace by means of the penitential rite. This is conceived as a process of shedding guilt, because there is such a limited understanding of what goes on in the sacrament. Such a procedure gives the impression that the person earns or buys his salvation by carrying out certain rituals. As a result, there is little understanding of the communal aspect. Even the contemporary effort at renewing the ecclesial or communal side of the sacrament is far from having achieved its purpose. People are too easily content with a juxtaposition of what are still individualistic procedures.

Since, as we said, the mind of the Christian masses is much more at home with the experience of the sacred and the religious than with Christian experience, the result has been a very magical kind of approach to the sacraments: both to the sacramental rites as such and to the realities signified by the rites. The experts in religious psychology say that this kind of "religious" experience is located at the level of having or possessing. The rite is quickly perceived to be something that gives us grace (itself an autonomous reality very difficult to identify). The rite takes on strongly magical overtones. In addition, when the approach to the sacraments, in terms of religious experience, is at the level of having or possessing, it is an easy step to reifying such sacramental realities as grace, merit, and sin.

In this context, it goes without saying that people attribute great importance to the rites, as though they were efficacious by themselves. Christian theology and Christian life in this period have paid a great deal of attention to the efficacy of the sacramental rite. We need only recall the classical theses on the causality and efficacy of the sacraments, on the ex opere operato, on validity and liceity, and so on. In themselves, these theses represented an effort to give expression to a very rich theological intuition, but when poorly understood they opened the way to certain theological ambiguities and distortions. People ended up isolating the sacramental rite from the factors which give it its authentic meaning. The result was a form of theological aberration.

The principal characteristic of this period in the Church's life, with its technical concept of a sacrament and its liturgical practice, was that it reduced the sacramental dimension of the Church to the sacramental rites. Similarly, since the element of proclamation and revelation of the Christian mystery as signified by the actions of the Church was more or less absent, the sacraments were often considered to be simply rites that produced grace. In this view, not only is the sacrament identified with a rite, but the function of the rite becomes simply to produce grace. The rite loses its function as revelation and celebration of the various dimensions of the Christian mystery. One function—that of producing grace— receives all the emphasis.

The foregoing analysis will suffice to bring out the major directions taken by sacramental theology and sacramental life, as an expression of the Church's faith in the second phase of ecclesiastical history. Such was the context in which the Church fulfilled its vocation as sacrament of Christ. Lest we pass only negative and anachronistic judgments on this period, it is good to note that this sacramental theology and sacramental life were the authentic expression of a culture and of a Church that was able to make that culture its own and carve out a place for itself in it.

Third period: From sacramental rites to the sacramental nature of the Church

We regard it as increasingly certain that with the conciliar renewal of the liturgy the Church is entering a new phase as far as the sacramental expression of its faith is concerned. It will be a quite different phase from the one we have experienced, which is still very much the current one in ecclesial communities but is gradually being left behind by anyone who enters into a new form of Christian experience. This new phase has been signaled by a key event—the theological renewal of Vatican II—that will lead to a new type of sacramental theology and a new style of ecclesial life. Just as the preceding phase was signaled by a key event—the elaboration of a technical concept of sacrament, which, as we have seen, dictated a whole style of sacramental theology and sacramental life for succeeding centuries—so the new phase is emerging from the thinking of the most recent Council.

More specifically, the starting point for this new look is undoubtedly the theological and pastoral renewal that Vatican II brought about in the area of the sacraments. We all know that Vatican II neither reaffirmed the old definition of a sacrament nor offered a new one. Its intention was not to correct or improve on the technical concept of sacrament. It took a quite different approach. It came to grips with the entire sacramental reality of the Church, but did so by way of the rituals, without directly touching on questions of the sacraments except by way of some general considerations scattered almost everywhere in its documents.

Some major principles governed the revision of the rituals. First of all, a liturgy of the word was introduced into each ritual, thus emphasizing the element of proclamation or revelation of the realities of faith that are signified in the sacramental rite. Next, the theological role of the Church as sacrament of Christ was highlighted. Finally, in order to bring to light the sacramental dimension of the various situations of human life, an attitude of adaptation and flexibility was introduced, which can be seen at work in the possibility given of choosing from among a number of readings and prayers and texts and even of composing prayers and texts that are better calculated to bring out the Christian meaning of the event being experienced.

Despite the importance of this reform of the rituals, we must not stop there in our reading of the theological renewal sponsored by Vatican II in the area of the sacraments. For the entire theological effort of Vatican II was geared to much more than a revision of rituals. By means of this revision, the Council gave a new direction to the sacramental life by helping the Church rediscover its sacramental nature and sacramental vocation. This is the key event in the new beginning upon which we are now engaged. The recovery of this truth which was so consciously present in the life of the primitive communities has helped the contemporary Church, and will help it even more in the future, to rediscover its vocation as sacrament of Christ.

The Church is becoming aware that it can respond to this vocation in many ways: by means of its entire visible reality, by its preaching of the gospel, by its celebrations, by the positions taken in Christian communities, by its institutions, by Christian charity, by forgiveness and fraternal admonition, by its involvements, and so on. Consequently, it is also becoming aware that the seven sacraments traditional since the Middle Ages are not coextensive with sacramental reality in its entirety.

It seems that this new awareness is of primordial importance for the course to be taken in the expression of Christian faith in coming generations. It will provide a new context for sacramental theology and the sacramental life; it will determine the orientations of a new phase in sacramental theology and practice.

In a description that is necessarily predictive or anticipatory, let us try to sketch the main lines of this new physiognomy of the sacramental life. The most important characteristic of the new phase in the Church will be a shift of emphasis. We will move from the sacramental rite to the Church as sacrament. Henceforth we will approach the sacramental reality much less by way of the rite or what we might call the sacrament-as-thing, the sacrament as an object in itself, the sacrament in the technical sense of the term, than by way of the global vocation of the Church. This is to say, as the Coffy Report puts it quite well, that "the question of the sacraments, of cultus, is not to be raised primarily at the level of the sacrament as means of grace for individuals, but at the level of a Church"[17] that expresses its own mystery by revealing to the world the meaning of life and history.

In the concrete, the shift will manifest itself in the importance assigned to a pastoral treatment based on meaning and not to the rite as such. The important thing will be the sacramental action of the Church much more than the celebration itself. Evidently it will be necessary to relocate the cultic celebration within the new approach. This is a task to which those in pastoral work will soon have to address themselves.

This shift in emphasis will deepen our understanding of the sacramental dimension of the Church as a whole, both in its institutional aspect and in its pastoral activity. For the Church fulfills its vocation to the extent that it leads men to recognize the gift of God in human reality; to the extent that it reveals to the world the meaning of existence, the universe, and history; to the extent also that it leads man into a realm of meaning he cannot enter by himself. Such an approach undercuts a narrowly conceived contrast of evangelization and sacramentalization. For the sacramental reality exists within the proclamation of salvation; it conditions it and gives it final unity. It is an intrinsic part of this proclamation of salvation, and without it the latter cannot be effectively carried out. It is therefore not possible to oppose two aspects of the Church's mission: the aspect of evangelization and the aspect of sacramentalization. To do so would be to raise again the problem that confronted the Reformers.

It is to be hoped that our concept of the Church's sacramentality will be broad enough today to keep us from falling back into the error of the sixteenth century which gave birth to two images of the Church: that of the Reform, with its Church of evangelization, of the word, and that of the Counter-Reformation, with

17. Robert Coffy and Roger Varro, *Église, signe de salut au milieu des hommes*, Lourdes, 1971 (Paris, 1972), p. 63.

its Church of the sacraments. In other words, the Church will effectively carry out its sacramental mission not only when it "celebrates the sacraments," but in and by every action that is intended as a proclamation of the realities of faith which the various Christian rites signify.

The development of the ecclesial dimension represents the recovery of something that was extremely important during the first phase of the Church's sacramental life. The Church will once again take priority in liturgical action. And this is quite as it should be, since we will be living more and more in a sociological context that is neutral or indifferent. In such a context, the vision faith has of life, the world, and history can no longer be taken for granted. Each Church will have to show the way by concretizing God's action so as to proclaim and make known to men the fullness of meaning contained in the message of Christ.

The point of departure will thus be very different than in a process that concerns only an individual. The focus is no longer on an individual who at this moment is seeking to appropriate some reality of faith and to secure a guarantee for himself, but on a Church which, conscious of its vocation, proclaims, makes real, and celebrates for itself first of all, and then for new Christians, some meaning that emerges from a specific human situation.

The highlighting of the ecclesial dimension of the sacramental event reduces the importance of the event as it affects the individual, but it should not make us forget the part man plays. For if the Church is to carry on its pastoral activity effectively, it must deal with the concrete. It must take as its point of departure some specific situation experienced by human beings. This is the so-called "anthropological dimension." It is not something really new, for it was present in good measure in the first and second phases; but in the coming phase it will be emphasized to a greater degree. For it is with a human situation—life, conflict, love, sickness, or death—as its starting point that the Church will proclaim the fullness of meaning which the message of Christ brings.

Finally, in this new phase the Church's pastoral action (and not the rite itself) will recover, emphasize, and articulate elements that were neglected in the second historical phase of the Church's sacramental life. One of these elements that the Church will recover and promote is that of proclamation-revelation. The stress on the efficacy of the sacramental rite, seconded by a magical approach to it, pushed this entire dimension into the background during the second phase. It will regain its place in the pastoral administration of the sacraments. We can even anticipate that it will take first place.

But proclamation or revelation of what? It is the proclamation of some aspect of God himself in his dealings with us; the particular aspect will be determined by the human situation in question. Thus a person who experiences some estrangement or conflict needs to be told that his God is not a vengeful God but a reconciling God who urges him to acquire the same attitude toward others as God shows him, since his vocation is to become fully an image of God. The revelation of which we are speaking is, then, the revelation of a whole area of meaning for a life.

The second element the Church will recover is that of concrete embodiment. The Church does not merely issue an intellectual proclamation of a message. Its aim is to lead human beings to *live* the message, to incarnate it in their lives. What we are speaking of here is the revitalization of the theses on the efficacy of the sacraments, but now in a context much less colored by magic, a context of embodiment and external signification, that is, a concrete anthropological context. The cultic celebration will undoubtedly continue to have its place, but it will not be coextensive with the sacramental reality. There will be a problem at this level: the problem of situating the ritual celebration within the overall pastoral activity of the Church.

Since the rite will no longer or, rather, should no longer be located at the level of having or possession (people will no longer go to the rite in order to acquire a little more of something) but at the level of meaning, it will have to keep clearly in view the eschatological dimension. For at every point in the pastoral ministry of the sacraments, it will be necessary to keep our sights fixed on an eschatological creation that corresponds to the first creation. And the aim of sacramental action is to reveal this eschatological creation as well as the dynamism that derives from it and leads us on to the attainment of it. Consequently, sacramental activity situates us in a dynamic perspective which is worlds removed from "the sacrament that is experienced," "the sacrament that bestows," "the sacrament that is received."

By way of conclusion to this historical overview, we can make the following assertions. First of all, there is no denying that in each of its historical phases the liturgy has been heavily influenced by its cultural environment. The life of the community was translated into a liturgy which, especially in the first phase, was careful to retain contact with the concrete life of the people. Furthermore, we must emphasize that the third phase, toward which Vatican II is directing us, is in part a return to the first. History shows that we had moved from a phase of creativity to a phase of uniformity. We are now in the process of reversing this direction. As we embark on this return, we will have to be careful above all not to give the back of our hand to the contributions of the second period. Despite its theological limitations and reductionism, this second period contains, as we have seen, values which are a permanent acquisition for sacramental theology and sacramental life.

4 — Theological Implications of the Renewal

It is an established fact that Vatican II gave rise to a liturgical renewal which found expression chiefly in the Constitution on the Sacred Liturgy and in the revision of the rituals for the sacraments. But despite its specifically liturgical character, the renewal has implications for the theology of the sacraments. Now, fifteen years after the renewal was set in motion, it is possible to single out three major points. First, we observe a shift of emphasis from the liturgy to the theology of the sacraments. Second, we observe that our classical theology of the sacraments has inevitably been undermined. Finally, the theologian is discovering a new task, which is to integrate sacramental theology once again with the whole of a renewed theology and sacramental practice.

A shift of emphasis: From the liturgy
to the theology of the sacraments

Given the abundance of the literature, it would be almost impossible to draw up a complete bibliography of the books, journals, and periodicals that have appeared on the liturgical renewal since the sixties. Almost every theme has been approached from various angles: the assembly, the community, participation, celebration, etc., etc., to say nothing of the numerous studies of each sacrament and ritual and of the efforts made in the area of liturgical song.

Despite the very wide range of publications that bring out the major values of the renewal and suggest various pastoral directions, pastors are still struggling to apply the renewal advocated by Vatican II. It might be said that just when they think they have succeeded, new problems arise which postpone the desired success. Some pastors even think the liturgical renewal has come too late. It might have met the expectations of pastors and Christian people if it had begun sooner. Priests are now facing new questions raised by the still massive request for the Christian sacraments and by the motivations offered to justify the request. Various questions have been asked about the minimum of faith required if a young couple is to be admitted to Christian marriage and if a newborn child is to be accepted for baptism.

As for the faithful, they are sometimes embarrassed when asked to justify the step they are taking. For example, the motives which used to dictate the baptism of children now have less influence. Original sin and the lot of the child who dies unbaptized are not what leads parents to the step of asking for baptism. There has been a shift of emphasis: people have moved from the periphery of the sacramental expression of Christian experience to the very heart of this expression. They have moved from the question of "how to celebrate the sacraments" to the question of "why the sacraments."[18] They have shifted their attention from the liturgy to fundamental sacramental theology. Consequently they ask much less about how to celebrate a sacrament on the occasion of this or that event in their lives than they do about the motive and meaning of such a sacrament. What is the specific role of a sacrament as compared with the expression Christian faith takes in various forms of Christian commitment? What does a sacramental rite add to the everyday life of faith?

Here we have a new set of problems calling for our attention and reflection even before we have found an answer to our earlier questions. The shift is especially striking among the young people who are preparing for marriage or having a child. Their main concern is not to prepare well for the ceremony of marriage or baptism; rather, it is to ask why have a baptism at all and why a Christian marriage instead of a civil one. It is in this sense that we can speak of a shift of emphasis in our contemporary pluralist context in which the realities of faith no longer go hand in hand with ordinary life. People are no longer asking about the various ways of celebrating a baptism or a marriage, for example, so much as about the function and meaning of these actions.

Despite the seemingly waning position of Christianity, we must be sure to see the positive results of the development we have been describing, a development people are living through

---

18. Raymond Didier, *Les sacrements de la foi: La Pâque dans ses signes* (Paris, 1975), p. 10.

without much adverting to it. A renewal is a reason for hope to the extent that it tackles fundamental questions. But that is precisely the kind of questions which the renewal of Vatican II is stimulating people to ask. We should rejoice, therefore, and be able to accept the challenge at the level at which it is really being issued, that is, less at the liturgical level than at the level of theology and specifically of the great fundamental questions which a sound sacramental theology will take up.

A theological identity undermined

The shift of emphasis from the liturgy to sacramental theology does not, however, solve the problem. On the contrary, it brings a new problem to light: that raised by a sacramental theology which is inadequate to answer the questions now being asked by the Christian people. The renewal of Vatican II is providing new directions for liturgy and raising problems of a theological kind. In addition, pastors who read the new rituals and apply them in the light of their theology often remain unsatisfied. Either the problem raised for them by the application of the new rituals cannot be located in the framework of the sacramental theology they know, as, for example, when a pastor asks about the function of the ritual celebration in relation to pastoral sacramental practice as a whole; or else they use the classical sacramental theology in order to assess the new sacramental pastoral practice, and then they feel uncomfortable.

This is the case with priests who, for example, ask the theologians to tell them whether or not a given form of communal absolution is valid. The answer they receive generally does not satisfy them, because the question and the answer are really not on the same level. This type of pastor judges a new pastoral practice in terms of classical sacramental theology and requires the theologian to formulate his response according to the same logic. But that is something the theologian cannot do, not because this question of a rite's validity no longer exists, but because the theologian interprets the new pastoral practice quite differently. He sees it as located more in the line of meaning and therefore of the connection with life. He sees it as outside the framework of classical sacramental theology. In sum, it can be said that the liturgical renewal of Vatican II is raising a new set of problems which classical sacramental theology cannot solve.

How explain this situation? As we see it, two things—the shift of emphasis that emerges from the change in the kind of problems raised for pastoral action and for theology from the beginning of Vatican Council II to our own day, and the theological analysis of the sacramental dimension of the new ritual—lead us to think that the Christian consciousness is in the process of resituating the sacramental dimension of Christian existence itself. The classical sacramental theology elaborated in the Middle Ages was coherent with the entire theology of the time. This coherence was to be found at the level of vocabulary, of course, but also at the level of the realities signified by the sacraments. In short, the approach to the sacraments that was conveyed to the Christian people corresponded to the approach to and conception of the Church, man, salvation, man's relation to God, and so on, as well as to the pastoral problems of the age. As a result, people felt at ease in this Christian universe. As we saw earlier, this sacramental theology that issued from the period of theological systematization which the Church experienced in the Middle Ages imposed an entire style on the sacramental theology and sacramental life of later centuries. It led to very concrete pastoral practices and stimulated reflection on a number of questions, such as the number of the sacraments, their validity, their liceity, the function and powers of the minister of each sacrament, sacramental causality and efficacy, and so on.

The theology of the sacraments that was elaborated in the Middle Ages was the vehicle of certain values and enabled the Church to carry out its vocation as sacrament in the society of the time. But since the theological, catechetical, and pastoral renewal inaugurated by Vatican II, the sacramental theology we call scholastic has been unable to find its proper place. When confronted with pastoral problems, it feels more or less awkward by reason both of its terminology and of its way of approaching the main points it has emphasized. What, then, is happening?

The coherence of sacramental theology with the whole of classical theology is being more and more undermined by the appearance on the scene of a new vocabulary, a quite different approach to the sacraments, and new problems. All this is emerging from the pastoral ministry and catechesis of the sacraments, as well as from the theological analysis of the new rituals; a further factor is the entire range of theological reflection in Vatican II. In point of fact, the Council did not elaborate a new theological synthesis of the sacraments. It simply provided a document on the liturgy and revised all the sacramental rituals. But we must take care not to err by minimizing the work of Vatican II in regard to the sacramental order.

A major threat to contemporary liturgical reform is the opinion that the Council simply revised the liturgy and the rituals. This it did do, of course. But by means of this reform of rituals and liturgy, it gave a new direction to sacramental theology, both in its vocabulary and in its approach. The result has been to make necessary a new kind of reflection on the sacramental expression of the Christian faith, and consequently on the pastoral ministry of the sacraments and on the sacramental life itself. It is in this sense that we can speak of the coherence proper to classical sacramental theology being severely undermined.

The undermining is due, on the one hand, to the very revision of the sacramental liturgy and the renewal of the pastoral sacramental ministry, and, on the other, as we shall see further on, to changes in other theological treatises such as ecclesiology, anthropology, and Christology. To use an analogy, it might be said that we are experiencing in theology what people experienced who exchanged their horsedrawn carriages for automobiles. Once the automobile had been bought, their old repair kit, wrenches and so on, were no longer of any use. May we conclude that they had no further need of tools? Of course not! They still needed wrenches and tools of all sorts, but new kinds of wrenches and other new tools. It is the same with sacramental theology. The new pastoral problems do not make sacramental theology useless, but they do make it aware of its limitations and inability to deal with hitherto unencountered problems at the pastoral level. They are an invitation to theologians to construct new theological tools that will enable them to appraise, direct, and challenge contemporary pastoral practice in regard to the sacraments.

The contemporary theological task: To restore coherence to sacramental theology

The new orientation of sacramental theology has not yet emerged with sufficient clarity from the work of Vatican II. This is a task for contemporary theologians, for once the rituals have been revised, there is a "new theology" to be discovered undergirding the reform. To grasp the timeliness of this task, it is undoubtedly useful to signal the novelty of the methods used by Vatican II in its reflection on the Church and on the sacramental life.

As far as the Church is concerned, the Council began by elaborating a theology of the Church, especially in its Dogmatic Constitution on the Church and its Pastoral Constitution on the Church in the Modern World. Postconciliar work has been on more of a practical level, such as the task of setting in motion the mechanisms which give concrete form to the theological idea that the Church is the entire people of God or that the hierarchy exists to serve the people, and so on.

As far as sacramental theology is concerned, the procedure of Vatican II was quite different. The Council called for the revision of all the sacramental rituals and gave the basic principles that were to govern this reform. The stage of revision was completed with the promulgation of the ritual for the sacrament of penance, *Ordo poenitentiae*, on December 2, 1973.

But this stage requires a further one that will involve theology to a greater degree, since in the stage of revision new theological principles were already at work. The theologian is thus bidden not to limit his vision to the practical and pastoral side, but to go further and apprehend the new sacramental theology that is at work. The task of today's theologians—an important one, since without it there is danger of falling short of the kind of liturgical reform for which the Council was preparing—consists in identifying the new approach to the theology of the sacraments, situating it in relation to its components, and giving it a new formulation. If this is not done, we risk simply exchanging one ritual for another without understanding the theological implications.

By its reform of the liturgy and by its reflection on the Church and its revision of the rituals, Vatican II did a great deal toward providing a new approach to the sacraments. But it must be admitted that reflection on other subjects likewise undermined the traditional approach to sacramental theology and made an extensive contribution to a new sacramental theology. The reason for this is simple enough. The sacraments are not isolated, autonomous entities, independent realities. They are at the center of Christian experience, and therefore the approach to them is very much conditioned by our conception of man, the Church, and Christ, and of the relations between all these. Theological reflection during the past quarter century, with its bases in the exegetical, patristic, and historical movements, has surely renewed the component elements in sacramental reality, at least in their formulation, by providing a new anthropology, a new ecclesiology, a new Christology, and a new conception of salvation. This is to say that a strong challenge is being issued to sacramental theology by the effort at renewal which the Church has undertaken in regard to its manner of carrying out its sacramental vocation and by the theological renewal of the component elements of the sacramental order.

This change seems important and even radical, to the point that we can consider Vatican II as a key event in relation to a new phase of sacramental theology, the pastoral approach to the sacraments, and the sacramental life. Just as the establishment of a technical concept of sacrament in the Middle Ages brought about a style of sacramentality that has lasted to our own time, so the renewal inaugurated by the recent Council will dominate a third phase of sacramental theology and sacramental life. For beyond the renewal of the liturgy and the rituals, there is a new conception of the sacraments that will infuse new life into many elements of the ecclesial heritage, propose new approaches, and restate the classical theses by locating them in a quite different context.

We must add that this sacramental renewal, both liturgical and theological, is far from being the result of a spontaneous generation. It goes back to Dom Guéranger in the last century and has continued to sink its roots with the help of numerous theologians like Dom Odo Casel. These theologians gave the impetus to a theological movement that went beyond the juridical and canonical aspects of the liturgy and located the liturgy at the very heart of the mysteries of Christ. The two theologians I have named also laid heavy emphasis on the theology of the mysteries. In short, their desire was to move beyond juridicism and place themselves on a level of meaning that lay within the mystery of man-in-Christ. It is against this background that the liturgical and theological renewal of Vatican II is to be understood.

The present task of the theologian, or the theological task of the Church, consists, then, in drawing from the liturgical renewal new principles for sacramental theology, giving this theology a terminology more in harmony with the language used by the Christian people and, above all, giving it a new coherence that takes into account the renewal in anthropology, Christology, and ecclesiology. It will also have to penetrate to the basic intuitions at work in the classical questions of sacramental theology, in order to incorporate these into a new synthesis. It goes without saying that this work represents a challenge to the entire Church. Faithful, pastors, theologians, and canonists must all accept it. It is desirable that the reform of the part of canon law which deals with the sacraments should grasp this new context and contribute to the success of the common task.

The task that faces today's theologians results from a fuller awareness of the historical and cultural conditions that affect Christianity. It is true that in and through Christ, God had addressed a definitive message to the human race. But even in its primary expression, the New Testament, the message bears the mark of a particular culture and a particular way of experiencing life in the world. Successive Christian traditions have endeavored to give the unique and decisive event of Christ's coming and presence in the world an expression that satisfied their contemporaries, using categories of thought familiar to them. Our age in its turn must do what previous generations did: give the sacramental reality a concrete form which is capable of stimulating the faith of our contemporaries by enabling them to express it in a truly adequate concrete way.

If this task is to be carried out, it seems important not to forget that the goal here is not merely to give the sacramental rites a suitable form. The meaning attributed to the sacraments has upon it the impress of the social and cultural situation of society at any given time. However, we do not want contemporary sacramental theology to deny the values of tradition. But the connection with tradition, far from acting as a brake, should rather direct and inspire our efforts to give the ever relevant, ever new event of Christ's presence in this world a form and content suited to the time and milieu in which we live. In a word, contemporary sacramental theology should turn its attention both to the relation between the traditional manner of understanding the sacraments and the traditional way of celebrating them and to the need of renewing the understanding and expression of them.

The Essential Components
of the Sacramental Order

Due to its richness and limitations, the new directions it suggests, and the entirely new problems it presents, the contemporary liturgical renewal is a challenge to classical sacramental theology and indeed to the whole Church, especially the theologians. Given this situation, we think it important to reflect on the discomfort felt in present-day sacramental theology in order that we may identify the deeper reasons for it and lay the foundations for a new sacramental synthesis. Such will be the purpose of this chapter: to try to find out why the familiar theology of the sacraments is ill at ease with the renewal.

We have already indicated the basic reason in our first chapter. Sacramental theology, more so perhaps than the other parts of theology, is not an isolated, watertight structure, but rather is heavily dependent on other realities that undergird it and may be called its components. In point of fact, sacramental theology, while linked to all the other areas of theology, has especially close ties with Christology, ecclesiology, and anthropology. Now there is no denying that these three treatises have profited most from the study and reflection stimulated by the recent Council. So true is this that we can speak of a new anthropology, a new ecclesiology, and a new Christology.

Such a statement calls for some explanation. Jesus Christ, the Church, and man will, of course, be always the same, but the grasp people have of them is very much bound up with contemporary culture, the development of exegesis, and the development of the human sciences and other disciplines. This is why on the one hand there is a challenge to classical sacramental theology from its components, and why, on the other, this theology will profit by a new inspiration and a new direction once its components are themselves renewed. In this chapter we shall see how Christology, ecclesiology, and anthropology have been approached in a new way and thereby have influenced sacramental theology.

1 — Christology and the Sacraments

The contemporary theological renewal would seem to have less impact on Christology than on ecclesiology and anthropology. And it is indeed true that there is less evidence in the official texts of Vatican II of a renewal in Christology than there is of the renewal in ecclesiology and anthropology, which were major concerns of the last Council. Nonetheless, we can justly speak of a new Christology, the influence of which is being felt in sacramental theology.

Renewal of Christology

The first major novelty of contemporary Christology is that it has regained a position of preference within the Christian mystery, and this in preaching and catechesis as well as in Christian practice. The Christianity of the years before the Council allotted little place to Christ. The religion of Christians was in practice focused almost exclusively on the divinity. The ongoing renewal, however, has shown a better understanding of the role of Christ in Christianity. From this flows a series of consequences for Christian life as a whole. The first is that there has been a decline in other devotions of every kind to the benefit of the person of Jesus.

Second, the new Christology is reviving the approach to Christ that was taken in the school of Antioch. As compared with the school of Alexandria, which followed the Prologue of St. John in starting with the divinity of Christ and then bringing out his humanity, the school of Antioch started with the humanity of Jesus and then moved on to his divinity.

Such an approach is in keeping with a sacramental conception of things. It starts with the sign and proceeds thence to what is signified. It starts with Jesus, a man apparently like any other, but then, thanks to the experience of faith, discovers what this Jesus is and means for us. No procedure could be more sacramental. One of the merits of Father Schillebeeckx is that he was able to locate the sacraments in relation to the Church, but even prior to that in relation to Christ.[1] In so doing, Schillebeeckx was making

---

1. Edward Schillebeeckx, O.P., *Christ the Sacrament of the Encounter with God*, tr. P. Barrett (New York, 1963).

his own the well-known saying of St. Augustine: *Non est enim aliud Dei sacramentum nisi Christus* (For there is no other sacrament of God save Christ).[2] Yves Congar has likewise revived this theological approach.[3]

Such an approach to Christology evidently tells us a great deal about Jesus, but it also tells us a great deal about how to approach the sacraments. Insofar as he is a sacrament, Jesus reveals God to man, man to himself, and man to God.[4]

To begin with, Jesus reveals God to man. In thus revealing who his God is, Jesus reveals the Father, the Son, and the Spirit to us. He shows that the encounter of man with him, Jesus, does not stop with him but leads the person on to the Father. "If you had known me, you would have known my Father also; henceforth you know him and have seen him."[5] The man Jesus likewise reveals who he himself is: the Christ and Lord, the Son of the Father, the Word of God. This revelation emerges clearly in the first Christological interpretations, those of the evangelists and the first Christian communities. Finally, Jesus also reveals to us that our God is a God who is Spirit. St. John is explicit on this point. Jesus makes known his Spirit, the Holy Spirit, by announcing his coming.

We should emphasize here the fact that Jesus as sacrament not only reveals the existence of the Father, the Son, and the Spirit, but in a sense expresses their presence. "He who has seen me has seen the Father," says St. John.[6] He is the presence of the Word of God and the presence of the Spirit, whom he calls his Spirit. In other words, Jesus is the human way of being God. We can see here the foundation and, in a sense, the application of the theological concept of symbol, and especially of real symbol, as developed by Father Rahner in an essay on the subject.[7]

In the second place, Christ, being a sacrament, reveals man to himself. It can be said that Jesus is the sacrament of man for man. For in knowing Jesus we not only know his Father and his Spirit; the knowledge of Jesus also reveals man to himself both in his present reality and under the aspect of his eschatological

---

2. *Epist.* 187, 34 (*PL* 38:845).

3. *Un peuple messianique*, p. 31.

4. Yves Coté, "L'expérience sacramentelle, rencontre de Jésus," *Communauté chrétienne*, vol. 7, nos. 38–39 (1968), pp. 209–10.

5. Jn. 14:7.

6. Jn. 14:9.

7. Karl Rahner, "The Theology of the Symbol," in his *Theological Investigations* 4, tr. K. Smyth (Baltimore, 1966), pp. 221–52.

future. To know Jesus is to come to know the future or, better, the eschatological image of man. This is St. Paul's theological perspective when he speaks of Christ as firstborn of all creation. This aspect of Jesus will be very important for the concept of a Christian sacramental rite.

Finally, Christ is also the sacrament of man for God. As firstborn of creation, Christ gives expression to man before God. As perfect image of man, Jesus is the prototypical, supreme, and perfect embodiment of man's response to the invitation which God extends to every human being that he should achieve his fulfillment as image of God. In speaking of Jesus as being the expression of man before God, there is need of many nuances and cautions. But it is nonetheless true that as sacrament of man for God, Jesus "says" man to God. In God's eyes Jesus is the perfect expression and embodiment of humanity. It is in this sense that we can assert him to be the sacrament of man for God. It seems important to call attention to this point: that Christ is not only the expression of God for man and the perfect image of God, but that he also embodies in God's eyes what man ought to be. This is not a new theology. We are stating the same thing when we say that Christ, in the name of the human race, gives glory to his Father, achieves man's reconciliation with him, and so on.

Present-day Christology is thus giving preference to an approach that is more existential and closer to the experience of the first witnesses of Jesus. It is a less metaphysical and more exegetical approach. In addition, contemporary Christology is taking cognizance of a great evolutionary vision and not restricting itself to the perspective of mankind's redemption from sin. Christ came to lead to its fulfillment a created world that had been made in him, through him, and for him. Everything has its place in the plan of God, who does not separate nature from grace or creation from redemption. Christ intervenes at a determined moment of human history to carry out the eschatological promises, thus producing the first fruits of what mankind as a whole is to experience. In the same way, he is the sacrament of man for man and for God.

Implications of the Christological renewal for sacramental theology and the sacramental life

The first impact of the Christological renewal on sacramental theology is to make us see the sacraments in the perspective of the sacramental nature of Christ himself. This means, first of all, an effort to view all the sacraments in their relation to the paschal mystery. The conciliar Constitution on the Liturgy is explicit on this point. The new rituals then give concrete expression to the same perspective by promoting the celebration of the sacraments within the celebration of the paschal mystery or at least in relation to this mystery.

The sacramental nature of Christ himself also determines certain functions the sacraments are to have. As a sacrament, Christ reveals God to man, man to himself, and man to God. In continuity with this, the Christian sacraments should reveal something of God to man and something of man to himself, both in his present condition and in what he is to be. In addition, they ought to give expression to man before God. It is in this framework that all Christian sacramentality becomes intelligible and should be developed. In all this there is a major change of perspective in the approach to the sacramental life, for the latter becomes much less individualistic and opens man to a whole universe of meaning which Christ alone can reveal.

The reference of every sacrament to Christ as the primordial sacrament not only enables us to discover many aspects of God—Father, Son, and Holy Spirit—and of man, but also gives us insights into the very meaning of a sacrament. We shall indicate some of these here and take them up again later on when we come to our attempt at a synthesis.

1. Christ as sacrament helps us to understand better various factors in what we call a sacrament. In Jesus as sacrament there is sign and reality signified. Jesus is not the Father, but at the same time he is more than a reference to the Father, more than a sign calling attention to the Father. In a sense, he is a new way of being for the primal reality which is the Father. We see this kind of relationship very clearly in the Church which, without being identical with Christ, is nonetheless for earthly beings the privileged mode of existence of Christ after his resurrection.

The same is true of a sacrament. If we want to grasp the full richness of the sacramental relationship, we must not identify it with the reality signified, with what we might call the primal reality. On the other hand, neither should we isolate it from this reality.

We may clarify this point by taking the Christian Eucharist as an example. When Christians gather to celebrate the Eucharist of the Lord, they do not simply relate themselves, as it were, to the communion of men with one another and with the Father, the Son, and the Spirit; they make that communion a reality in a certain measure. They express in a new way the communion of Father, Son, and Spirit.

2. As a sacrament, Christ is seen to be the one who takes the initiative in revealing himself and revealing what man is and who God is. The apprehension of the signified reality (*res significata*) is not the fruit solely of man's personal development. That is to say, man does not by his own resources attain to a true perception and grasp of what Jesus, the Christ and Lord, is. It is God who, through Jesus, takes the initiative and reveals himself to man. Jesus is explicit on this point when he says to Peter after the latter's confession: "Blessed are you, Simon Bar-Jona! For flesh and blood has not revealed this to you, but my Father who is in heaven."[8]

God's initiative, given concrete embodiment by and in the community, will therefore be an important factor in the sacrament itself. If this factor is absent or at least neglected, the sacrament is in danger of being misunderstood, and dubious pastoral practices may be the result. Sacramental theology must therefore make plenty of room for God's initiative and be able to integrate this with another factor, which is the personal assent of the believer.

3. In continuity with the second point just made, we must call attention to the element of faith that is necessary for every sacramental action. The realm of meaning into which the sacramental sign leads us is not accessible by mere personal reflection; it can be perceived only in the experience of faith.

It is perfectly true that Catholic theology has never ceased to emphasize the necessity of faith for the validity, that is, the very existence, of the sacraments. But the reaction of the Reformers who, in the eyes of Catholic theologians, had exaggerated the role of faith in the sacramental event, caused these theologians to underscore the objective character of the efficacy of the sacramental rite. The result was that most manuals of sacramental theology paid little attention to the sacrament as an expression of personal faith, as a faith-event. Happily there has been a rather sudden change of climate in recent years, as numerous publications show.[9]

4. There is a further aspect. As a sacrament Christ has a sig-

---

8. Mt. 16:17.

9. On this point, see, for example, the Constitution on the Sacred Liturgy, no. 59; M.-D. Chenu, "Foi et sacrements," *La Maison-Dieu*, no. 71 (1962), pp. 69–78; L. Villette, *Foi et sacrement* (2 vols.; Paris, 1959–64).

nificance for all of mankind. He is a part that represents a whole: for God he represents the whole of mankind, and conversely for mankind he represents the totality of God. The sacraments in turn acquire this same value, which some exegetes and theologians have expounded in terms of "corporative person."[10]

It is, moreover, a property of signs and especially of symbolic actions that they refer to a totality. To clarify what this means as applied to a sacrament, let us take marriage as an example. The Christian celebration of marriage takes place at a very precise moment in the life of the young couple. At the same time, however, the celebration relates to the entire life of the couple. The particular moment embraces the whole life; the whole life is concentrated in the particular moment, just as mankind was concentrated in Christ. This point is important if we are to understand that the influence of a sacramental action is not exhausted in the moment of celebration.

5. Finally, the sacramental nature of Christ as model for every sacrament highlights another important factor, that of revelation and embodiment. If Christian tradition has thought of Christ as being a sacrament, this is because, on the one hand, he revealed what he really was in relation to God and man, and, on the other, he embodied this same revelation.

2 — Ecclesiology and the Sacraments

Ecclesiology is one of the areas of theology most affected by the conciliar renewal. It must be said, however, that the roots of the renewal were put down well before Vatican II, for contemporary reflection on the Church is in fact the fruit of a great movement in ecclesiology that began with Mohler in Germany at the beginning of the last century.[11] This new movement sought to go beyond the extrinsicist and sociological approach which the theology of Bellarmine had spread abroad throughout Western Christendom, and to take a new approach to the Church that would pay more attention to its internal life.

The movement has a long history.[12] After a timid and hardly

---

10. Bas van Iersel, "Some Biblical Roots of the Christian Sacrament," in E. Schillebeeckx and B. Willems (eds.), *The Sacraments in General* (Concilium 31; New York, 1967), pp. 5–20; cf. pp. 15–20.

11. Johann Adam Möhler, *L'unité de l'Église ou le principe du catholicisme d'après l'esprit des Pères des trois premiers siècles* (Unam sanctam 2; Paris, 1938).

12. See the study of Etienne Ménard, *L'ecclésiologie hier et aujourd'hui* (Essais pour notre temps 1; Bruges–Paris, 1966).

noticed beginning in Mohler, this type of thinking won attention at Vatican I in the form of a schema or position paper that was put aside at the time. Since there was need of haste, the Fathers of that Council limited themselves to only a part of the picture of the Church, namely papal infallibility, which did not seem to fit in well with the new current of thinking in ecclesiology.

Despite this setback, at the beginning of the twentieth century new theologians began the work again. Conscious of the theological values this type of thinking represented, they continued their studies, drawing largely on the writings of the Church Fathers. During the thirties, the idea of the Church as people of God began to spread. It can be said that from the forties on there was an abundant literature in ecclesiology that sought to express the mystery of the Church as seen from various sides and in the light of various trends. Thus 1943 saw the publication of the Encyclical *Mystici Corporis* of Pius XII, and this in turn occasioned numerous studies, in particular the two volumes of Sebastian Tromp, S.J., who was Pius XII's theologian in this area.[13]

On November 21, 1964, the Fathers of the Second Vatican Council presented Christians and the world with a new ecclesiology that was in continuity with the movement of Mohler and the nineteenth-century Tübingen school. This ecclesiology showed a very different face of the Church and gave the Reformers of four centuries earlier a very different kind of reply than the school of Bellarmine had shown and given at the beginning of the seventeenth century. The Dogmatic Constitution on the Church was a historic event, for in it for the first time, after twenty centuries of ecclesial life, the Church stopped to describe itself to itself and to tell the world as well what it is. This is not the place to present a new treatise on the Church, but it is important for our purpose to indicate the major lines of this theology and their implications for the sacramental order.

Renewal of ecclesiology

The most truly novel thing about Vatican II is that it gave us an ecclesiology. Previously Christians had lived the reality of the Church without making any great effort to identify and define it. Another very important aspect of the conciliar renewal is that it has presented the Church in a sacramental perspective, and this chiefly in terms of its relation to Christ as the primordial sacra-

---

13. *Corpus Christi quod est ecclesia* (Rome, 1946 and 1960).

ment. The Dogmatic Constitution *Lumen gentium* is explicit on this point.[14] Once again, this new notion has produced an abundant literature in recent years.[15]

The development of the theme "Church as sacrament of Christ" is something of a latecomer to sacramental theology. The delay is readily explainable, however, when we advert to the context in which the theology of the sacraments took shape. As is commonly known, at the time when sacramental theology was being developed, medieval Christendom lived with little attention to any world outside itself. Since the distinction between the Church and the world had been eliminated, it was inevitable that people should lose the idea of the Church as a sacrament and should focus their attention on the individual sacraments.[16]

In addition to the sacramental dimension that runs through the entire conciliar ecclesiology, the Constitution *Lumen gentium* has introduced some new perspectives that likewise influence the way in which the sacraments are approached and understood. First of all, a clear distinction is made between the Church and the Kingdom, thus preventing us from assigning an absolute value to the forms and means the Church has adopted in order to bring men into the Kingdom. This relativization of the Church does not detract from its soteriological role, but it does force us to be aware that the sign is not the reality signified and that the sign will always be ambiguous, since by its nature it hides as well as reveals the reality it signifies. Once we have grasped this, we will perceive more clearly not only the relative character of the Church and its entire pastoral activity but also their full importance.

A second ecclesiological perspective emphasized in *Lumen gentium* has to do with the participation of all Christians in the mission of the Church as such, a participation now being manifested by the establishment of new parochial and diocesan structures. This perspective, though still new, has begun to take hold in some ecclesial milieus. Where it is accepted, it creates an entirely

---

14. See nos. 1, 9, and 48.
15. On this topic the following works are suggested: Yves Congar, *Un peuple messianique*, especially pp. 57–98; Edward Schillebeeckx, *Christ the Sacrament of the Encounter with God*, pp. 47–89; idem, *The Mission of the Church*, tr. N. D. Smith (New York, 1973), pp. 43–50; the Coffy Report: Robert Coffy and Roger Varro, *Église, signe de salut au milieu des hommes*; Gustav Martelet, "De la sacramentalité propre a l'Église ou d'un sens de l'Église inséparable du sens du Christ," *Nouvelle revue théologique* 95 (1973), pp. 25–42; idem, *Idées maîtresses de Vatican II* (Foi vivante 105; Paris, 1969), pp. 77–131.
16. See J. J. von Allmen, *Prophétisme sacramentel* (Neuchâtel–Paris, 1964), pp. 12, 15.

new mentality: the Christian people regard themselves no longer as consumers of ecclesial goods administered by the hierarchy but rather as themselves responsible for the mission of the Church and for bringing the Church to its fulfillment. This new outlook will obviously influence our approach to and understanding of the Christian sacraments.

Another point that is important for our subject emerges from the sacramental perspective underlying the ecclesiology of Vatican II. The Church defines itself here in terms of signification, and not of power, possession of truth, and holiness. This new orientation will surely influence sacramental theology and the pastoral ministry of the sacraments. Vatican II has emphasized the interior, spiritual, and mystical side of the Church, even while always relating this to the external and visible aspect. Thus in the first chapter of the conciliar Constitution, the Church is presented as a mystery of communion: communion of men with one another, and communion with the Father, the Son, and the Spirit. But this communion takes a concrete visible form; in other words, it is signified by that assembly of Christians whom we call the people of God. This point is taken up in the second chapter of *Lumen gentium*.

To sum up: Vatican II has struck a balance between the two fundamental aspects of the Church which have given rise to different approaches and ecclesiologies. In the conciliar presentation, the Church is seen as structured in accordance with sacramental theology, that is, as having both a visible and an invisible aspect; or, to use a more traditional expression, the Church comprises both sign and thing signified.

Finally, in its reality as sign or sacrament, the Church is the means by which God gives concrete form to his action among men. This is a point to which we shall have to return. Let us say for the moment only that the Church is the sector of mankind which, in the name of the entire race, responds to God's initiative. Thus it becomes the sacrament of mankind.

Implications of the renewal in ecclesiology
for the sacraments

These new ecclesiological perspectives will necessarily influence sacramental theology and the sacramental life. Even though it is rather difficult to anticipate what all these changes will be, we can even now point out some of them.

First of all, the fact of resituating ecclesiology in relation to the whole of Christian theology will force a new vision of the sacraments, since these will no longer be seen as isolated actions but as the activity of the Church. Here we can take and adapt a familiar theological adage: "The sacraments make the Church, and the Church makes the sacraments." This integration of the sacramental rites into the great sacrament which is the Church (the Church itself always being seen in relation to Christ, the primordial sacrament) prevents these rites from being isolated any longer; they are seen rather as the prolongations and more particular embodiments of the great sacramental sign which the Church is. The result will be greater attention to the sacramental nature of the Church, to its pastoral activity, and to its specifically sacramental actions.

More importantly, the sacramental rites will acquire their meaning to the extent that they are sustained by a pastoral action that endeavors to be sacramental. Thus we shall see a shift of emphasis from the sacramental rite to the sacramental nature of the Church. This shift will raise new problems for sacramental theology, such as the problem of the place and importance of the rite in relation to a pastoral ministry of the sacraments that embraces not only the moment of the rite but the time before and after as well.

The integration of the sacraments into the great sacrament which is the Church will likewise have consequences. While the personal aspect of every sacramental action will not be minimized, the sacraments will be regarded as the expression of the entire community and not as rites administered by a single minister to a single believer. As a result, there will be less emphasis on the individual aspect, the personal upbuilding, the benefit the individual receives. Such a theology evidently harks back to the patristic tradition that saw clearly how a sacrament was to be defined first and foremost as an event for the community and not as an event for the individual.

Consequently, the Church will no longer be perceived as the place where a sacramental rite occurs, for it now becomes the subject that performs the rite, the principal agent of it, because as sacrament of Christ it is the Church that has the vocation of proclaiming, carrying out, and celebrating the plan of God in each human life and specifically in each major situation of life.

We can already glimpse here the new problem for sacramental theology and the pastoral ministry of the sacraments: to relate the sacramental action of the community to the personal step being taken by the individual. To say that the sacraments have an important ecclesial dimension, as the Constitution on the Sacred Liturgy does so often, is to give priority to the Church or community. And this holds good not only chronologically but at the level of meaning, inasmuch as the action of the community signifies, embodies, and concretizes the initiative of God. The ecclesial or communal aspect of a sacrament is therefore to be understood only in the light of the Church's sacramental vocation to carry on the work of God.

The emphasis on the fact that the Church's mission belongs to the entire Church and that it is wholly a mission of ministry (to use phraseology that is still somewhat new) will lead to changes in the sacramental life. The liturgical renewal and revision of the rituals are opening the way to this participation in the Church's mission. But let us not believe that this participation will come easily. On the one hand, Christians who are aware of the opportunity to give expression to their lives in the sacrament will suggest and even demand rites, formulas, and actions that will not always be in accord with current regulations for liturgy, and this despite the sincerity of their desire to participate. On the other hand, pastors, realizing this desire for participation and being heirs of a certain liturgical tradition that embodies great Christian values, will hesitate to allow Christians to take these initiatives.

There is therefore a work of Christian education to be done both among pastors and among the faithful. It is important to emphasize here the work pastors do among the faithful. We can draw inspiration on this point from a saying that was applied to bishops of Christian communities in the patristic era, and with the help of it draw up a whole program. The bishop was regarded as "guardian and promoter" of the liturgy. In this contemporary period of renewal, these two aspects of the pastor's role remain as important as ever.

The pastor will have to be the guardian of the liturgy in order that the sacramental expression of the faith will not be cut off from Christian tradition and that it will be protected against the temptations emanating from the worlds of entertainment, society, the secular. He will also have to take on a new role, that of promoter of the liturgy. Undoubtedly pastors have always been such promoters. But this role is going to acquire a new importance. For it is not a question simply of providing the habitual agents of liturgy—organist, liturgical committee, etc.—but of promoting a sacramental life and a sacramental liturgy that take into account all the orientations of the liturgical and sacramental renewal.

Finally, the emphasis of *Lumen gentium* on the interior and

46

spiritual side of the Church is making Christians uncertain of how to evaluate the sacramental rites, which they associate chiefly with the external side. By laying exclusive emphasis on the visible and external aspect of the Church, people run the risk of looking upon the sacramental rites as a form of magic; on the other hand, excessive emphasis on the interior aspect of the Church can lead to a failure to understand the meaning and importance of the sacraments. Sacramental theology must therefore endeavor to situate the sacramental rites within an ecclesial life that has due regard for both aspects.

3 — Anthropology and the Sacraments

From the very nature of sacramental reality, it is fully to be expected that sacramental theology and the pastoral ministry of the sacraments should depend on the kind of anthropology that reigns in the Christian consciousness. Now, with the biblical renewal and the theological endeavors of Vatican II as formulated in the Pastoral Constitution *Gaudium et spes*, the Christian consciousness is in process of establishing for itself a new conception of man.

Such a new anthropology makes uneasy those who take a preconciliar approach to the sacraments. On the other hand, it leads to and undergirds new implications for sacramental theology and the sacramental life. It is worth adding that Christian anthropology, inclusive of the concepts of salvation and earthly realities, is the area of theology which, along with ecclesiology, has been most influenced by the conciliar renewal. This influence is exerted not only at the theological level but at the practical level of new mentalities. We can conclude that this component of the sacramental order will profoundly affect sacramental theology and the pastoral ministry of the sacraments.

Renewal of anthropology

In the next section we shall sketch out the main lines of contemporary Christian anthropology as this has emerged from the renewal of exegesis and from the renewal sponsored by Vatican II. We shall then go on to speak in detail of the theological concept of man, and therefore to the view taken of the role of the sacraments in Christian life.

New directions in the anthropology of Vatican II

1) Man the image of God

Contemporary thought has made its own the very traditional theological statement that man is the image of God. This theological formula, used in Genesis, was taken up by the Fathers of the Church, among others by Athanasius of Alexandria in his treatise *The Incarnation of the Word.*

> Thus he created all things from nothing through his own Word, our Lord Jesus Christ. . . . He was not satisfied to create human beings as he had all the animals unendowed with reason that live on the earth, but instead made them in his image by giving them a share in the power of his own Word.[17]

St. Thomas makes extensive use of this theology of man as image of God, and Vatican II likewise employs it in its Pastoral Constitution *Gaudium et spes.*[18]

From this theological tradition comes the idea that man is an image of God, a reflection of God, a sacrament of God. It is a very optimistic view of man as compared with the pessimistic view promoted by the sacramental theology and sacramental life of the period preceding the present renewal.

At this point a question arises: How is this theology of man as image of God to be interpreted? The Constitution *Gaudium et spes* points out three essential elements in this kind of Christian anthropology: the relation to God that makes the human being capable of knowing and loving him who is man's creator and end; the relation to the world that makes man "lord of all creatures on earth," because as an incarnated spirit man expresses himself by means of science, the tool, and the machine; and the relation to other human beings, apart from whom he cannot live and act to the full.[19]

In order to be and become an authentic image of God, man must cultivate right relations to God: a God who is a Father, a God who is Love, a God who wants man to succeed. He must also cultivate right relations to the world in which he lives; he must remain lord of creation. Man is a creator of meanings. He is the master and not the slave of science, the machine, and the tool. Finally, he must cultivate right relations to his brothers and sisters.

These three kinds of relations are essential to the fulfillment of man. They are constitutive of his being, since if one of them is

---

17. *Contre les paiens et Sur l'incarnation du Verbe*, ed. P.-Th. Camelot (Sources chrétiennes 18; Paris, 1947), p. 213.

18. Nos. 12–22.

19. Jean Mouroux, "Les grandes lignes d'une anthropologie," in *L'Église dans le monde de ce temps* (Unam sanctam 65; Paris, 1967), 2:236.

distorted or missing, that is, if the relations of man with God, nature, or other human beings are deformed, he cannot be fully an image of God. This anthropology is bound to have important consequences for the sacraments, since the latter will have as their purpose to reestablish human beings in this threefold relationship.

2) A historical vision of man

By its emphasis on the concepts of nature and supernature, medieval theology left a static conception of man as its heritage. And yet the context in which Christianity originated was characterized by a quite different view. In fact, well before Christ, the mind of Israel laid emphasis on the historical dimension of man. In Genesis this idea is admittedly not yet central, but it is nonetheless implicit in all that Genesis says about man. Full clarity comes with the New Testament, for now we have before us the perfect and definitive image of God, the "image of the invisible God," as St. Paul calls him (Col. 1:15). Jesus is thus the normative image for man, who is called to become like it. Here St. Paul also makes a further dimension known to us: the image is an eschatological one. It already exists in germ within man, but it must attain to its full reality through a progressive formation.[20]

During the first Christian centuries, there was a gradual movement away from this biblical and, in particular, Pauline conception of man. There was a shift of emphasis. In addition, the primarily historical understanding of Christian existence was altered by an emerging ritualism, by a Platonic dualism, and by the juridicism that reigned in Roman private law. Western anthropology, like the rest of theology for that matter, felt the increasing domination of an essentialist thinking that concentrates on objectivity. Fortunately, contemporary Christian thinkers are reacting against this approach and restoring to its proper place the historical dimension of human life.

This dimension acquires sharper contours when we add to it the communal and relational aspects of man. In this new anthropological vision, it is impossible to conceive of man attaining to his salvation by means of an individualistically interpreted relationship with God. No, man is part of a history, and the fabric of history is woven of relations within the human community. Such a vision of man is quite different from the individualistic vision fostered

---

20. A. Ganoczy, *Devenir chrétien* (Paris, 1973).

by the sacramental life of recent times; it emphasizes a strongly communitarian and personalist side of human life. Given this approach, our perspective on the sacraments changes drastically.

3) A dynamic vision of man

Because it takes into account the historical dimension, contemporary theology also offers a dynamic vision of man. Contrary to an approach that regarded him as passively assigned to one or other state, the newer approach sees him as sharing in an evolutionary process that involves the kind of progress and setbacks inherent in any evolution. Far from being passive in this evolutionary process, man enjoys a certain control over the movement. That is something we should expect, given his condition as image of God. As God's image, he possesses within himself a source of energy that gives him a certain control over his own evolution. The theology of the incarnation that we find in Athanasius of Alexandria is very illuminating on this point, for it does not limit the real significance of the dogma of the incarnation to the man Jesus but sees it as affecting all of mankind, or man as such.

The human greatness which Athanasius highlights in his thinking on the incarnation of the Word is not simply a conclusion implicit in his theology of the incarnation; it is part of the very message of the dogma of the incarnation. For, according to Athanasius, our faith in the incarnation of the Word tells us that the man Jesus was so energized by the Spirit of God that he must be said to possess the divine nature; and this same faith tells us that man as such is energized by a source of energy that comes from God.

In other words, the human person possesses a dynamism that is divine in origin and enables him to become in his concrete life what he really is, namely, the image of God. This idea of man taking charge of his own fulfillment is intelligible only in an eschatological perspective. In fact, through the entire pastoral treatment of the sacraments, it is good to keep before us the eschatological creation that corresponds to the original creation.

4) A unified vision of man

The theology of the generations preceding our own has accustomed us to a dualistic conception of man. Body and soul were the essential elements of the human composite. Vatican II avoided taking any specific philosophical position and was content simply to maintain the unified vision of man that is presented in the biblical tradition. In this tradition, man is not a composite of body and soul; he *is* body and he *is* soul. An analysis of the concepts of the biblical anthropology which in its broad lines was taken over by Vatican II shows no division in man. On the contrary, the realities designated by the three concepts of *nephesh, basar,* and *ruah* are never parts of man that are to be set alongside other parts; the reference is always to man as a unity and totality, but envisaged from different angles.

This anthropology is set over against that of the Greeks, which exerted a strong influence on Western theology. In the biblical view, the soul is never regarded as superior to the body; the body and the flesh as such are never indicated to be the causes of sin; finally, man is not regarded as finished and closed, but as open, even in his corporeality, to the eschatological future that Christ has made possible for him.

Consequences for the theological concept of salvation

The new understanding of man both in his relation to himself and in his relation to God and the whole of creation (including the eschatological perspective) compels us to reevaluate the concept of salvation, which is likewise so important for sacramental theology. Basing ourselves chiefly on Father Congar's work,[21] we shall make three main points. First, we shall outline the biblical idea of salvation; then we shall give a summary overview of the major ideas of salvation in the Christian tradition; and finally we shall attempt a contemporary interpretation of salvation. Salvation is a very complex reality, and in the course of history it has received a number of theological formulations, the first being that given it in the religious experience of Israel.

1) Biblical concept of salvation

The word "salvation" and its derivatives come from the Greek verb *sōzein,* which is used in the Greek translation of the Bible (the Septuagint) to translate a set of Hebrew roots that all relate to the same basic experience. According to the *Dictionary of Biblical Theology,* "to be saved is to be taken out of a dangerous situation in which one risked perishing. According to the nature of the danger, the act of saving manifests itself in protection, liberation, ransom, cure and health, victory, life, peace."[22] The idea of keeping the being intact and safe, of maintaining its existence,

---

21. *Un peuple messianique,* pp. 101–64.
22. Colomban Lesquivit and Pierre Grelot, "Salvation," in X. Léon-Defour (ed.), *Dictionary of Biblical Theology,* translation edited by P. J. Cahill (2nd ed.; New York, 1973), p. 519.

seems to be a common denominator.

The idea of salvation underwent a development, of course, in the religious consciousness of Israel and in that of the new people of God, the Church. Subsequent to its experience of liberation from oppression, Israel reflected that such a liberation presupposed the intervention of someone stronger, a savior. The savior and liberator might be a human being, but Israel soon saw that the only real savior must be Yahweh who raises up human liberators within his people. Such were Abraham, Moses, the Judges, and others. Thus the idea of salvation quickly came to include a reference to the triumph of God's power as exercised on behalf of his people. This explains, on the one hand, the striking connection between the words "salvation" and the "strength" and "power" of God, and on the other hand, the attitude of Israel which proclaimed the power of God whenever it wished to announce salvation.

In Israel the concept of salvation has three main characteristic notes. Salvation is something temporal; it is also collective; and it has an eschatological finality. The liberation or salvation wrought by Yahweh is part of the people's history. It is thus something temporal. When Yahweh intervenes, when a human liberator appears on the scene, it is in order to free Israel from oppression by an enemy, or from some dread or distress. It is to be observed that the liberation is most often collective, that is, bestowed upon the entire people, although it of course affects individuals as well. The prayers of the Psalms mention individuals, such as David, who become aware that Yahweh has saved them. But the awareness of salvation also comes at the gathering of the people. Thus salvation will take the form of gathering the exiled and dispersed in order to make of them a people whose duty it will be to worship Yahweh. The liberation here has a very precise purpose and will take place, in its full form, on the day fixed by Yahweh. Thus, in the Old Testament the experience of salvation already has a temporal, a spiritual, and above all an eschatological aspect.

In the New Testament, Jesus comes as Savior, and his contemporaries realize that this is what he is.[23] With this statement as his starting point, Yves Congar sums up the soteriological aspect of Jesus' work in the following three statements.[24]

23. See Jean Giblet, "Jésus, Messie et Sauveur d'après les Évangiles synoptiques," *Lumière et vie*, no. 15 (1954), pp. 45–82.
24. *Un peuple messianique*, pp. 114–39.

1. Even though Jesus rejects any kind of temporal messiahship for himself, his word and actions nonetheless have a political impact. This is fully consistent with the anthropology of the time; since the latter knew nothing of a Platonic duality of body and soul, it rejected a salvation restricted to souls while the world around them would be neither saved nor changed.

2. Jesus saves from sin, from the wrath of God, and from the second death. St. Paul lays heavy emphasis on this aspect of salvation. He develops the point in continuity with the prophets who had linked salvation with a judgment and had proclaimed the "Day of Yahweh" that would bring God's real victory and the real salvation of his faithful. At the same time, however, Paul is careful not to give the impression that salvation will come only after death. He maintains the dynamism deriving from the eschatological expectation, but at the same time he manages to keep a fine balance between three aspects of salvation: salvation already made real in its principle, salvation now becoming a reality for us, and salvation in its final, eschatological form.

3. The saving action of Jesus includes bodily healings and the restoration of authentically fraternal relations among all human beings. Bodily healings occur frequently in his life. If we are to understand them, we must see them in the perspective of the salvation he brought and of the anthropology of the time. The healings tell us that man's wholeness is part of Jesus' mission as Savior and therefore of Christian salvation. The message of Jesus concerning salvation embraces the body too. But to avoid misinterpreting this statement, we must also see the healings in the context of biblical anthropology, for it is only there that they acquire their full meaning. In the Bible, the body "is the whole man in his sensible manifestation. It is worthy of note that when Jesus heals a bodily member, the 'salvation' affects the whole man and not just the isolated member."[25]

In addition to curing bodily illnesses or infirmities, Jesus had as one purpose of his salvific mission "to incorporate into the human community and the religious community of Israel those who had been excluded from them."[26] This included the Samaritans, the tax collectors, the lepers, and all those whom the Israelite aristocracy regarded as despised and outcast. In all this Jesus sought

---

25. *Ibid.*, p. 128.
26. *Ibid.*, p. 129.

to create fraternal relationships while reminding men that earthly cures and acts of liberation were not everything and did not constitute the entire ultimate destiny of man.

2) The major interpretations of salvation
in the Christian tradition

The biblical concept of salvation, which we have described in a summary, not to say schematic, form, was subject to a process of acculturation. It was represented in varying ways according to the state of the society and culture to which Christians belonged. We shall sum up here the conclusions of Father Congar.[27]

1. In antiquity, emperors and kings soon provided traits and images for expressing the role of Christ as Savior. The testimony of iconography is unequivocal on this point. As Lord and Master of the universe, Christ attracted to himself the idea of *salus publica* (the welfare of the nation or people), which was borrowed from Roman imperial ideology in order to express the unlimited universality of the salvation won by Jesus. This in turn fostered the conception of Christendom as an empire of which Christ was the supreme king. Consequently, roles proper to the emperor were attributed to Christ.

2. The Middle Ages in the West interpreted salvation "as a grace of communion with God and of spiritual freedom." This implied the restoration of proper order between man and God, and therefore the conquest of this-worldly suffering and all that comes between man and his true likeness to God. This conquest was effected amid struggle and difficulty, for "people were very conscious of the demon's active presence." Moreover, men were inclined to see sickness, epidemics, hailstorms, and calamities of every kind as due to their sins and as a punishment inflicted by heaven. There was need, therefore, of doing penance, multiplying indulgences and pilgrimages, and invoking the intercession of numerous saints in order to obtain mercy from God and so to attain salvation, that is, to avoid hell and shorten purgatory.

3. This popular view of salvation persisted beyond the Middle Ages. According to Father Congar, it still accounts for many forms of behavior and dictates the way many Christians approach the sacraments. It is also burdened by elements of folklore and superstition, just as it has taken its special coloring from various currents of spirituality, such as pietism and Jansenism. Rather clearly, this conception of salvation motivated missionaries from the sixteenth

27. *Ibid.*, pp. 145–54.

to the nineteenth centuries as they endeavored at any cost to save souls, that is, snatch them from hell by means of baptism. Another source of the missionary impulse was the related theological problem of children who die unbaptized.

4. The concept of salvation that held the field in the nineteenth and twentieth centuries has been elucidated with remarkable clarity in a study by Sister Elisabeth Germain.[28] Father Congar calls attention to four essential characteristics as identified in this study:

1. *Consciousness of a dramatic choice:* salvation or damnation. Damnation means hell, demons, fire. And this for ever.

2. *Salvation is identified with the redemption of souls:* the rest of the created world has little or no place here. *The perspective is quite individualistic.* What room is there for the assertions of Scripture about the universe?

3. *This salvation-redemption is seen as something already accomplished which the faithful are to make their own by means of certain specific actions: religious actions and practices which are in large measure determined by the clergy or in which the clergy act as intermediaries,* such as confession, First Fridays, almsgiving, the last sacraments. In missions and retreats people are told what they must do to avoid hell, shorten purgatory, and merit heaven, or, in brief, "to save their souls."

4. *Hardly anything is said of the salvation of the unevangelized.* In missions to the pagans the situation is comparable, except for the realism required by circumstances and the part played by the activities of civilized society. Concerning the latter I have already had something to say; it was not, of course, neglected in the countries where the faith had been long established.[29]

3) A contemporary interpretation of salvation

It is to be expected that the renewal of Christian anthropology will lead to a new approach to salvation. In summing up the essential characteristics of this new approach, we shall turn once again to Father Congar's analysis, which emphasizes the following traits.[30]

First of all, the contemporary idea of salvation flows from the consciousness man now has of himself in relation to "others." Not only is he becoming aware of new dimensions to the world, new socio-cultural spaces; he is also becoming aware of his historical and evolutionary course through time. "We have passed," says

---

28. *Parler du salut? Aux origines d'une mentalité religieuse* (Théologie historique 8; Paris, 1967).

29. *Un peuple messianique,* p. 149; italics added.

30. *Ibid.,* pp. 149–54.

Father Congar, "from the idea of the world beginning in 5199 B.C. . . . to a Teilhardian vision of a vast cosmogenesis and anthropogenesis." Seen in this perspective, men are living a history of which they are also the makers, a history which, in Teilhard's vision of it, has a global meaning that has its place somehow in the plan of salvation. In addition, biblical and patristic[31] research has enabled us to recover an eschatological understanding not only of every individual but of the entire history of mankind; this eschatological understanding imbues Christianity with a sense of unqualified hope for the world.

To be a Christian, then, one must be a human being, that is, take an active and involved part in the building of the world and in the great movement of liberation which is coextensive with the very history of mankind. Such a conception challenges the ideas and modes of behavior of centuries past in which people tended to justify the status quo too easily and to presume that those in authority were right, thus justifying as well economic and social inequities, encouraging the oppression of the lowly, and explaining why there was so little concern for the advancement of man, for liberty, for the struggle against injustice.

Another source of challenge to the preconciliar conception of salvation is the new vision of the relations between the spiritual and the temporal, the natural and the supernatural. As is well known, the question of the spiritual-temporal relationship was very important to the very concept of Christianity, especially from the Middle Ages on. A Platonic dualism had led to the question of the relationship being raised; then, in the Middle Ages, the question took on a new importance in the special context created by the confrontation of the two powers, temporal and spiritual, that is known as the dispute between *sacerdotium* (priesthood) and *imperium* (empire). In that context, the spiritual was superior to the temporal and tended to subordinate the latter to itself. This view of things, given greater currency by the situation that prevailed from the Middle Ages down to our own day, cast discredit on nature and earthly realities, to the point where Christians hardly acknowledged that there existed a world outside the Church.

This view was inevitably undermined by the development of the sciences, modern movements, and man's consciousness of

---

31. See, for example, Henri Lassiat, *Promotion de l'homme en Jésus Christ d'après Irénée de Lyon* (Mame, 1976).

the values inherent in himself and in nature. Consequently, the Council enabled Christians to take a giant step forward in their attitude to earthly realities. Vatican II put aside a certain ecclesiocentrism and acknowledged the cohesion, autonomy, and truth proper to earthly values. In so doing, the Council moved beyond the kind of Augustinianism for which there is no authentic justice, no authentic virtue apart from grace and the theological virtue of charity.

This new vision also challenges a certain conception of the natural and the supernatural. It is a fact that after a good deal of discussion in connection with *Gaudium et spes*, the conciliar Fathers avoided the terms "nature" and "supernature," thus giving notice that they were henceforth locating the debate within a different problematic from the one which had provided the framework until then.

In setting aside the opposition between earthly and other-worldly values and in reaffirming the eschatological aspect of the Kingdom, the Fathers of Vatican II made it clear that the world and the Church are no longer to be thought of as radically opposed but rather as moving together toward the Kingdom. Father Congar says explicitly: "The Kingdom of God embraces both the Church and the world. When it attains its eschatological fullness, it will make the two one; more accurately, it will unify whatever in each of them is from God and for God."[32]

The Pastoral Constitution *Gaudium et spes* is an important witness to this kind of thinking. Here are two expressive passages.

We have been warned, of course, that it profits a man nothing if he gains the whole world and loses or forfeits himself [cf. Lk. 9:25]. Far from diminishing our concern to develop this earth, the expectancy of a new earth should spur us on, for it is here that the body of a new human family grows, foreshadowing in some way the one which is to come. That is why, although we must be careful to distinguish earthly progress clearly from the increase of the kingdom of Christ, such progress is of vital concern to the kingdom of God, insofar as it can contribute to the better ordering of human society.[33]

This new manner of relating earthly values to the realities of the Kingdom underlies the principles which the same Constitution provides in regard to relations between faith and culture.

In their pilgrimage to the heavenly city Christians are to seek and relish the things that are above: this involves not a lesser, but rather

---

32. *Un peuple messianique*, p. 153.
33. *Gaudium et spes* (December 7, 1965), no. 39; Flannery, p. 938.

a greater commitment to working with all men towards the establishment of a world that is more human. Indeed, the mystery of the Christian faith provides them with an outstanding incentive and encouragement to fulfill their role even more eagerly and to discover the full sense of the commitment by which human culture becomes important in man's total vocation.[34]

Such a presentation of the relations between the temporal and the spiritual in a new context leads us to rethink the Christian concept of salvation. At a meeting at Bievres in 1972 of regional and diocesan delegates for the ecumenical movement, Danièle Leger said: "What meaning can the word 'salvation' have if, in the concrete, religious institutions and groups and religious bodies are not involved in a struggle to make the idea of liberation plausible to our contemporaries?"[35] People no longer believe in a salvation that is unconnected with the great concerns of the day, in a salvation that amounts to a negation of the progressive effort by which men liberate themselves from their alienations, oppressions, and ills. On the other hand, they realize that salvation includes far more than the partial liberations which often preoccupy men so exclusively.

It is doubtless premature to attempt a full description of the new vision of salvation that has been elaborated under the influence of anthropology and the new conception of the relations between the temporal and the spiritual. Nevertheless, we can at least point to certain characteristic traits that enable us to discern the kind of interpretation the contemporary Christian consciousness is giving to the idea of salvation.

The concept evokes, first of all, the idea of man in his totality and fullness. It is a totality that makes obligatory an effort to build a better world here below, but also a totality that includes the eschatological future. Then there is the cosmic dimension of redemption, or the link between man and the universe.

We saw above that recent anthropology has adopted as a framework the notion of man as image of God. It is to be expected, then, that the theological concept of salvation will adopt the same framework, since salvation means the complete fulfillment of man. Now the anthropology of *Gaudium et spes* explicitly links the theme of man as image of God with the category of *relation*: relation of man to himself, to nature, to other human beings, and to

---

34. No. 57; Flannery, p. 961.
35. In *Unité des chrétiens*, no. 7 (July, 1972), p. 20; cited in Congar, *Un peuple messianique*, p. 154.

God. To become an image of God, man must establish right relations with all of these. This, then, is what being saved means: to attain fulfillment in harmonious relations with oneself, with the environment, with others, and with God.

Such an approach makes no distinction between the temporal and the spiritual; it includes temporal values. It also fosters social and political involvement and the promotion of purely spiritual and cultural values. And just as the image of God in man is something that evolves, so salvation is not something given and acquired once and for all. It is always something that still lies ahead; it is always eschatological. There is thus a constant process which never allows man to rest. He must be always moving toward his salvation, toward the attainment of the bright image Jesus constantly holds up to him. More concretely, man's salvation comprises his own fulfillment, the fullest possible development of his body, his potentialities, his personality. As the parable of the talents indicates, man must make what he has bear fruit; he must make full use of the riches he has. If he is to do this, he must discover these riches and use the means of developing them, thus preventing his talents from being buried.

Such a task can be carried to completion only in collaboration with three essential factors: the environment (including nature), other human beings, and God.

The rapid growth of the great cities has very quickly made it clear that man must establish a harmony with nature and his environment. This need is keenly felt nowadays and is expressed chiefly in a return to nature and the countryside. Preceding generations knew how to use the environment profitably. Our ancestors lived their lives in harmony with nature and the environment, with the climate and seasons. All of these things influenced their life, their domestic architecture, and so on.

Since man, the image of God, is a relational being, his relations must extend to other human beings. This involves a whole program of human relations at the level of both the individual and the community. At the individual or personal level, man must develop a more than superficial kind of communication with those around him. This is fundamental if he is to "say" and express himself. Thus he must develop both his capacity for expressing himself and his capacity for listening so that the other too may communicate himself. At the community level, this perspective leads to a whole program for social justice and human brotherhood at the level of institutions, the school, and the family, and at the level of the great economic, political, cultural, and other values.

Finally, the integral salvation of man cannot bypass his religious dimension. Christ presents us with a new image of the Absolute. In the time of Jesus, there were a number of religions which conveyed the picture of a God who was jealous of his power and often quick to anger and vengeance. Christ, however, shows us a God who is a kind Father, compassionate, considerate, and loving. It is this God whom man is urged to know; it is with this God that he is to cultivate relations. The idea is a very simple one, but in practice it is not an easy one to live by. Man is so inclined to picture God according to his own prejudices and projections that he must constantly struggle to retain the image of his God as a good and loving Father.

Since salvation means the totality and plenitude of self-fulfillment, man may not neglect any of these relationships if he is to be saved. Christian faith evidently intervenes here to broaden man's perspectives. In the Christian perspective, man's salvation includes numerous forms of fulfillment at various relational levels. It also includes the great liberation from the hold that death has on man. For only faith in Jesus Christ opens up new horizons for us in regard to life and death. Salvation includes all this: liberation from the enslavements man creates for himself, and liberation from the great enslavement of death as well as from the dreadful prospect of annihilation that death brings with it. And all this is perceived in the context provided by an anthropology of man as image of God, and especially of God's image as something that is to be made fully real in man.

Implications of the renewal in anthropology
for sacramental theology and the sacramental life

It is quite clear that this vision of man and Christian salvation is, on the one hand, a challenge to the conception earlier centuries had of the sacraments, and, on the other hand, offers new orientations with the help of which that conception can be redefined. Let us try to indicate some of these directions.

Generally speaking, the new anthropology raises questions for a sacramental theology and a sacramental practice that are marked by distortions. Thus, too "pinpointing" a conception of the sacraments does not fit in well with an anthropology that sees man in an evolutionary perspective. Similarly, too individualist a conception of the sacraments fits in poorly with an anthropology that develops the relational side of man.

What is to be said, then, of a view that attributes something of a magical efficacy to the sacraments, when this view is judged from the standpoint of an anthropology that, while not denying the dynamism of spiritual values, emphasizes the activity proper to man in his progress and fulfillment? We may add that an approach to the sacraments which looks only at spiritual goods and values is opposed to a unified conception of man and the universe in which spiritual values are embodied in temporal and material values.

We can also indicate some more specific implications for sacramental theology of the renewal in anthropology. To see man as image of God is to take into account his historical and developmental aspect. Man is in a certain sense already the image of God at his birth, but he is called to become that image more fully. This means that in sacramental theology, as in other areas of theology, we must keep in mind the eschatological creation that corresponds to the first creation.

In this perspective the sacraments acquire a new function, a new role in man's fulfillment and attainment of his salvation. Their function is to make known to man the image of God which he is called upon to realize in himself; and their function is also to help him achieve this realization. A sacrament does not provide this image automatically or in a static way; rather, it directs man toward this image by first of all revealing it to him and then showing him that his entire life must be directed toward making it real in himself.

It seems very important to indicate this new context for the sacraments, since otherwise there is danger of not grasping their importance and necessity. True enough, if we start with the Christian perception of man as an evolving image of God, we cannot talk of the absolute necessity of baptism or the importance of confirmation or the Eucharist in the same way as people did in a different anthropological context. But in this matter we must proceed with a good deal of prudence lest we fall into errors that might well adulterate Christian thought. We cannot say that the sacraments of Christian initiation are no longer necessary, but we can say that the problem of their necessity is no longer being put in ontological or logical terms or in terms of physical necessity.

In this new way of looking at the sacraments, baptism is not a rite which by itself can bestow some part of the reality we call salvation. It becomes first and foremost an action of God through his Church, an action which has for its function to reveal to man his true image (his eschatological image) and to help him make that image real in himself. Thus the message of Jesus is the message of a new creation, a total vision of man, and not a message that broken pots are to be put together again by means of the sacraments. The thesis on the necessity of the sacraments thus retains its full importance, because the sacraments tell man what he is and what he is called to become; on the other hand, it enables us to see that the question of the age for baptism is secondary. Baptism certainly remains necessary for salvation, because it is the process by which God, through his Church, makes known to man the meaning of his life, a meaning which is the same as the meaning of Christ's life before him, and urges him to respond to this invitation throughout his life. Baptism has this function, not in order to satisfy a whim of our God, but in order that each individual may be saved.

In summary, it can be said that the sacraments are necessary both from the viewpoint of God and the Church and from the viewpoint of man. It is perhaps paradoxical to say that God needs the sacraments. As St. Thomas has shown, God has certainly not linked his grace exclusively to the sacraments (*Deus non alligavit gratiam sacramentis*), but he has indeed made the sacraments a privileged means of revealing himself and signifying his presence. This is why the sacraments can be said to be necessary from God's viewpoint. As for the Church, the sacraments are the great means it has of structuring itself and building the Kingdom. The old adage is still valid: The sacraments make the Church and the Church makes the sacraments. Finally, each sacrament is necessary for man in order that he may discover God's plan for him and his place in the Church and be able to give expression in the Church to his response.

In this new anthropological context, the sacraments of Christian initiation, like the other sacraments, have for their purpose to lead man to discover all the dimensions of his existence as well as the source of the new life that dwells in him and his human brethren. Thus it is easy to understand that a sacrament is not limited to a precise moment in a life, the moment of its celebration. The moment of the celebration certainly remains important, but we must keep in mind that a sacrament also has a before and an after!

Contrary to the static conception of man that led to a "pinpointing" mentality with regard to the sacraments and considered them to have an efficacy in themselves, the new anthropology brings a more dynamic vision of man. It must be made clear, of course, that such a vision does not deny an initiative on the part of God who presides over man's development. But the divine initiative does not reduce man to a passive recipient of salvation via the sacraments, nor does it imply that man wins his salvation in exchange for fulfilling certain conditions.

A final point deserves special attention. I refer to the relational aspect of man as image of God; this aspect is harmoniously integrated into the new concept of salvation. We have seen that the idea of man as image of God relates man to himself, others, nature, and God. We may ask to what extent sacramental theology and the overall sacramental renewal have been influenced by this idea. They have certainly profited from it to the extent that they have acquired a better context in which to view man's relations with God. The picture of God that emerges from the present-day sacramental liturgy is much more in harmony with the picture Jesus gives us of his Father. The idea of a threatening, vengeful God who is bent on chastising is almost wholly absent.

On the other hand, sacramental theology and the sacramental life do not seem as yet to have responded adequately to the other kinds of relations man has, although these are no less essential an element in his salvation. The need for such a response opens up interesting avenues for exploration; indeed, the exploration is a necessity if we want the sacraments to speak to the whole man. At first sight, certain sacraments lend themselves more readily than others to this kind of thinking. The first that comes to mind is the sacrament of reconciliation; we might add baptism, the anointing of the sick, and the Eucharist. The new *Ordo poenitentiae* does reflect the new outlook, though hesitantly. It supposes a concrete kind of reconciliation that embraces reconciliation with oneself, with nature, with one's brothers and sisters, and with God. There is still room, however, for emphasizing the personal and cosmic aspect of man which a good sacramental rite should be able to envisage and express.

The new vision of Christian salvation is also a challenge to sacramental theology. The new Christian consciousness of a salvation that includes the temporal dimensions of man has as one of its consequences that people no longer know how precisely to situate the sacraments in their lives. They no longer believe in sacraments that have effects only on the soul, without any relation to man's earthly life. Furthermore, has there been any successful integration of the sacraments with other ways of expressing the Christian faith? Have we grasped the specific character of a Christian's socio-economic involvement in the name of his faith in Jesus Christ, as compared with the specific character of a Christian's giving expression to this same faith via the baptism of his child or via the Sunday Eucharist? And, assuming that we do put our finger on the specific character of each, can we harmoniously integrate the two ways of expressing the faith? The question is not an easy one, because the persons involved in the situations include both conscientious, involved Christians and pastors who are concerned to safeguard the properly sacramental dimension of Christian life while being at the same time anxious to integrate with it the social, political, and economic commitment of a large number of Christians.

4 — Conclusion

Our intention here is not to summarize the main points of this chapter, but simply to call attention to some principles as the basis of which, in our view, sacramental theology should be developed. We wish also to call attention to some aspects of sacramental theology that need to be especially emphasized in our day.

First of all, our sacramental theology must lay special stress on the Christological and ecclesial aspect proper to the sacraments. It must be shown that we can understand the sacraments only in the light of Christ and the Church. Father C. Traets, S.J., brings out the importance of these requisites quite well when he writes:

The sacraments should be seen as a prolongation of the sacramentality —in an extended sense of the term—of Christ and his Church. We speak of "sacramentality in an extended sense" in order to indicate that we are no longer dealing directly with ritual, liturgical celebrations. But the sacramentality in question is not therefore any the less real, for Christ and his Church are the efficacious manifestations of the salvation God offers us. And it is important to realize that priority belongs to the sacramentality of Christ and the Church, not to the ritual sacraments. This is clear from the way St. Paul and the Fathers use the term *mysterion—sacramentum.*

The whole purpose of the sacraments is to give concrete form to the sacramentality of Christ and his Church. More precisely, it is through the sacraments that we become more and more fully Christians in and through the Church. They give us an orientation that influences us in a special and decisive way to lead our lives and fulfill our mission through union with Christ in the Church.[36]

In the second place, sacramental theology must give greater attention to man himself, his experience, his social, cultural, and other environments. Consequently it must profit by the contributions the human sciences are making to our understanding of symbolic action, ritual behavior, the experience of transcendence, the ways of celebrating life, and man's need to express himself. This anthropological approach will help in situating the sacraments within the whole range of symbolic actions and of man's celebrations of the events of human life, be these secular or religious.

Finally, these three approaches—the anthropological, the Christological, and the ecclesial—will help Christians situate the sacraments in relation both to man and to Christ and the Church. There is no denying that a certain kind of sacramental theology and sacramental practice have contributed to the real isolation of the sacraments, so that they have been celebrated on the periphery, as it were, of ordinary Christian life. The Christian has had to leave his secular life behind in order to find God in a sacramental celebration that takes place in a completely different world. Today's Christian has a keen sense of the value of the concrete world in which he lives; as a result, he feels like an alien in the world of sacramental celebrations that do not really touch him deeply.

The sacraments have suffered from a similar isolation from the Church and Christ. It is cause for rejoicing, then, that contemporary sacramental theology is realizing more fully that the sacraments are actions of Christ and the Church. This means that in and through the sacraments Christ is making his own earthly life present and operative for us. In regard to the Church, it means that the Church is not merely placing at our disposal the realities signified by the sacraments, but is itself the one uniting us to Christ in the fundamental situations of our human life.

It seems evident that the renewal in Christology, ecclesiology, and anthropology (with this last including a new approach to salvation) has consequences for sacramental theology. On the one hand, the renewal explains why many Christians are uneasy with the sacramental life and the pastoral treatment of the sacraments. Many Christians who are sharing in a real, even if not always fully conscious, way in the ongoing renewal of theology are in-

---

36. C. Traets, S.J., "Orientations pour une théologie des sacrements," *Questions liturgiques* 53 (1972), p. 107.

creasingly ill at ease with an approach to the sacraments that is based on an ecclesiology of power and on a static and fundamentally negative, not to say erroneous, conception of man. A Christian whose understanding of man, the Church, and salvation has not developed since Vatican II will not grasp the reasons for the changes in the contemporary pastoral treatment of the sacraments. His image of the Church continues to be an image of a fussy, interfering institution.

On the other hand, the renewal will help us to see the implications of the new rituals and, above all, to extract from sacramental practice and the liturgy of the sacraments a theology that is better integrated into the Christian mystery as a whole.

3

Sacramental Theology:
An Essay in Synthesis

The considerations that follow are a response to the challenge of which we have been speaking. They aim at offering a sacramental theology just as the conciliar renewal produced an ecclesiology. We have been seeing how the realities—Christ, the Church, and man—which form the basis of the sacramental system are the ones that have profited most from the conciliar renewal. So true is this that the coherence with the rest of Christian thought which sacramental theology had earlier acquired has now been extensively undermined, and this at the level both of vocabulary and of approach and content. The present task of the theologians is to give sacramental theology a new coherence in relation to and as part of the Christian mystery. That was the challenge issued earlier. That is why the present chapter is diffidently offered as an essay that will be completed, to its profit, by further work and research.

This new synthesis of sacramental theology does not claim to be wholly novel, for it has as integral elements values which twenty centuries of life and thought have acquired in the area of the sacramental expression of Christian experience. Our aim, therefore, is to retrieve the valid elements in the ecclesial heritage and to grasp the basic intuition behind the major theses of classical sacramental theology. Behind the theses on validity and liceity and on matter and form, which no longer exercise the influence they did of old, we can detect a fruitful intuition which, when reformulated in contemporary language and situated in the present ecclesial context, will always continue to provide a sound way of evaluating, directing, and criticizing any particular sacramental expression. Profiting from the theological renewal of certain parts of the Christian mystery, namely, Christology, ecclesiology, and anthropology, this new synthesis seeks to integrate the sacramental order with the totality of the Christian mystery, and especially with the essential foundations of that mystery.

Such a goal is inevitably too comprehensive for the limits of the present essay. But it is the goal toward which we are moving, even while conscious from the outset of the limitations of our work. We hope that all those concerned with the problems of sacramental theology and the pastoral ministry of the sacraments will be able profitably to go beyond what is offered in this essay.

This theological essay is organized around four major themes. The first is a consideration of the theory that is basic to the sacramental order: the theory of Christian sacramental symbolism; here we shall be reflecting, as theologians always have, on signs and symbols. The second point we shall consider is the *actants*[1] in sacramental activity, namely the Church, Christ, and man. Two further aspects—the functions and the dimensions of sacramental activity—will complete our theological synthesis by showing the significance and role of all sacramental life.

1 — The Foundational Theory: Christian Sacramental Symbolism

Sacramental realities, and specifically those we call "the sacraments," are evidently not autonomous and independent entities. We may even indulge in paradox and say that the sacraments do not exist. That is to say, they do not exist after the fashion, for example, of objects in a laboratory that can be catalogued, dissected, and analyzed. What really exists is Christ, the Church, and man, all of whom perform actions that have sacramental value. But the factor that enables us to discover a sacramental dimension in objects and actions and even in events and persons is precisely what contemporary theologians call Christian sacramental symbolism.[2]

The principles of Christian sacramental symbolism

All of sacramental theology—that which deals with Christ

---

1. We ask the reader's pardon for using this technical term. In our opinion, it expresses the reality better than do the terms "actor," "agent," or "effecter."

2. See Viateur Boulanger, Guy Bourgeault, Guy Durand, and Léonce Hamelin, *Mariage, rêve—réalité* (Héritage et projet 14; Paris, 1975), pp. 83–93.

the primordial sacrament and with the Church, the great sacrament of Christ, and that which analyzes sacramental actions[3]—has two foundations: the symbolizing mind of man[4] and the capacity of things, events, and human persons to point to a meaning beyond themselves.

Let us consider these two foundations separately. First, we shall reflect on the second of them, that is, the capacity of earthly things to signify something other than themselves or something other than what they show at first glance. We know that this principal holds not only for material entities but for persons, situations, and events as well. This understanding of earthly reality was taken for granted in the Middle Ages. Father Chenu has developed this point in a book on St. Thomas Aquinas.[5]

Though the situation may seem to have changed, we still look at reality in the same way. In fact, the psychological sciences are even helping us to rediscover this principle. For in the view of experts in these disciplines and even in the view of everyone who unconsciously acts as psychologist or sociologist, things, persons, modes of human behavior, and situations signify something beyond what they express at first glance. The situations of life, the actions and behavior of man are a language we must know how to interpret. This is the case because the human person and his activity and even material things have a density or fullness of meaning that a language reflective of corporeal things does not completely express. We may say, in short, that all human situations, events, persons, and even material things have a symbolic value— that is, they have a second meaning that goes beyond their first meaning.

The other principle, which is closely linked with this one, has to do with the structure of man's mind and with his grasp of symbolism. Admittedly, a certain conception of man that is influenced on the one hand by the value set on work, productivity, and effectiveness, and on the other by an exaggeration of the role of reason to the detriment of imagination, has led people to believe

---

3. "Sacramental actions" refers to the seven sacraments recognized as such ever since the Middle Ages, to the sacramentals, and to all the other activities of a Christian that are sometimes described as "sacramental."

4. Boulanger et al., *Mariage, rêve—réalité*, p. 83.

5. M.-D. Chenu, O.P., *Toward Understanding Saint Thomas*, tr. A.-M. Landry, O.P., and D. Hughes, O.P. (Chicago, 1964).

that twentieth-century man is technique-minded to the point that he is no longer capable of entering the world of symbols generally and of the sacraments in particular. This supposed outlook means an impoverished concept of reality in which things and persons along with their actions are reduced to their external manifestations. Father De Jong says: "The *homo technicus* of our age tends to make physical reality the supreme and even unique and unqualified value (physicalism)."[6] Such a frame of mind has led to a consistent overvaluation of material reality. As a result, the person accustoms himself to regarding things only as material which man is to shape by his work. In addition, the progressive ignoring of the reality of the symbolic dimension has led to an attitude of distrust toward the idea of symbol as applied to the sacraments. This way of conceiving reality allows no room for the transparency proper to the symbol, a transparency which gives entry into the world of the invisible and on which the whole sacramental principle rests.

But this supposed scientific and technological mentality of contemporary man does not go very deep. We need but push a little and we discover that behind a very real pragmatic and utilitarian outlook there is hidden a deeper attitude to reality that looks to what lies beyond earthly things and that grasps the symbolic meaning of reality. Here we are in continuity with the man of antiquity and of the Middle Ages who lived in a world of symbols. For the men of those times, water was not simply H_2O or water in terms of its physical components. It was certainly that, but the material reality was enriched with a whole range of symbolic meanings: water as life-giving power, as source of life, as agent of destruction. It is this symbolism, of course, that provides the basis for the sacramentality of baptism.

It would be interesting to investigate the ways in which the symbolic outlook of present-day man finds expression. We might explore the various domains, tastes, and interests of modern man in order to bring to light the need he feels of penetrating beneath the surface of things and getting past the sheer materiality of the world around him. Poetry, for example, or song, leisure, the return to nature, and the interest in antiquity seem to be privileged ways in which man can give rein to his propensity for symbolism.

It is of interest to observe that Christian sacramental symbolism

---

6. J.-P. De Jong, *L'Eucharistie comme réalité symbolique* (Cogitatio fidei 65; Paris, 1972), p. 31.

is based on a human symbolism shared by all mankind. It can be said that we will find two levels of interpretation. One is of a very general kind and is shared by all men; it is what we might call human symbolism. The other is more specific and depends on the faith of the interpreter; this is Christian sacramental symbolism. Independently of our faith, we all make an initial reading of life, nature, and ourselves, and inevitably of others, too, and the events and situations of life. This reading applies the principles common to all symbolism, namely, the capacity of things to say something more than they express at first glance and the mental attitude that enables man to go beyond the brute materiality of events and life. All human situations, persons, nature, and so on have a symbolic value in the sense that they manifest a deeper reality than appears at first sight. A point to be emphasized here is that the symbol not only carries the mind onward to the symbolized, but also contains something of the symbolized; in other words, the symbol is a locus of both revelation and presence for the symbolized or signified.

Once he looks at reality with the eyes of faith, man changes registers, as it were. He continues the symbolic reading of reality, but now he does it with a new lens that enables him to see something more. The new lens is more than a filter which changes the color of things. To continue this comparison from photography, we might say that the new lens enables him to see hitherto invisible details, a new meaning, an unsuspected landscape.

In order to make such a new reading, it is important to locate the word properly, since it is the word that acts as the lens, makes the change of register possible, and introduces us into the realm of Christian sacramental symbolism. The word in question becomes the form of the sacrament. It is to be noted, however, that it acts as form not solely at the moment of what is called the essential sacramental rite but throughout the whole sacramental process and the sacramental life generally. Sacramental symbolic language, like all symbolic language, uses symbols that have their context in a culture. This fact raises the problem of the universality of language, its regionalization, and its evolution. It is a known fact that at a given period of their history certain words become more heavily freighted with meaning and emotional connotations. Christian symbols are no exception to this phenomenon of acculturation. They must therefore be re-evaluated in the light of their new meanings. The liturgical renewal of Vatican II has confirmed the need of such an effort.

Our reflections bring us to another point for comment. It is good to emphasize here the existence of various levels of sacramentality in connection with one and the same human situation. For example, there are two different levels of sacramentality expressed by persons not yet fully believers who are preparing for marriage and by two profound believers who are advancing toward the celebration of a sacramental marriage. The two couples experience and express a sacramentality but in very different ways. One type of pastoral practice is beginning to take this difference into account. Some young couples are ready for a sacramental celebration of their marriage but do not judge it necessary that the celebration take place within the framework of the Eucharist. Here is a first step which seems to lead to the recognition of different levels of sacramentality. It is to be desired that pastors advance further along this line.

The Church has applied these principles of Christian sacramental symbolism to the particular situations which gave birth to the seven sacraments that have been recognized as such only since the Middle Ages. In fact, however, the principles apply to practically all the situations of life. By defining the Church as the sacrament of Christ, Vatican II has considerably extended the application of these principles. We find ourselves somewhat confused by all this, since we had been accustomed to recognize as sacramental only seven privileged situations. We must therefore make our own this new view of the Church as a sacrament, in order that we may interpret the whole of human life in sacramental terms.

It seems important, therefore, to acquire a good understanding of this religious symbolism that gives the Christian the sacramental outlook he needs. It is quite difficult to situate Christian sacramentality and therefore the pastoral ministry of the sacraments except in this context of symbolism. If we do not thus locate it, we are in danger of failing to understand the present liturgical renewal, which attributes so much importance to the different situations of life as ways of bringing man to a fullness of meaning that goes beyond what is seen at first glance. In classical theology this importance is expressed in terms of "the matter of the sacrament." A remote matter indeed, but matter nonetheless. Let us say right now that the matter of a sacrament is the human situation to which it is related. The contemporary liturgical effort to connect the sacraments with life seems to be an attempt to concretize the theological principle just enunciated. As a matter of fact, the principle is not a new one; it simply reiterates the Thomist intuition embodied in the categories of proximate and remote matter.

These two principles—man's symbolic outlook and the capacity of things, men, and their situations to signify more than they say at first glance—are the foundations of sacramentality. It is with them in mind that we must enter the Christian sacramental universe. The person who is conscious of these two principles and lives by them daily will not be able to approach life, love, failure, sickness, and death without trying to get at their deeper significance. The Christian also finds that the service offered by the Church takes on a whole new meaning when it is seen in the perspective of Christ as sacrament and of the Church as sacrament. It is on these two principles that the whole theory of Christian sacramental symbolism is based. A sacramental theology and a pastoral approach to the sacraments that ignore this theory also risk opening the door to the influence of the magical mentality; this is a snare which the sacramental practice of the Church has not always managed to avoid.

The progressive discovery of the principles
of sacramental symbolism

We know today that the Christian communities of the early centuries did not always have a very specific notion of what a sacrament is and that they gradually discovered, through the situations of their life, the implications of the Christian mystery. On the other hand, it is easy to see from the history of the sacramental life in the Church that the sacramental principles just discussed were the very ones that presided over the growth in awareness and over the development of the sacramental expression of Christian experience. Let us take as examples marriage and the anointing of the sick.

In the first centuries of the Church's history, the Christian rite of marriage was for practical purposes nonexistent. Christians who married celebrated the event according to the rites and customs of those around them. Very soon, however, sacramental principles began to exert their influence. People became aware that human marital love possessed a fullness of meaning that went beyond simple cohabitation and procreation. The Christian, accustomed as he was to interpreting things and events symbolically, made his own faith-inspired reading of this human situation. He discovered that marriage, that is, conjugal life, was a privileged occasion for the Church to make explicit certain aspects of the paschal mystery, namely, the face of a God who is Love and the commitment of the Christian couple to reflect that countenance in their life together. It was then that there developed out of an initial simple blessing a liturgy of marriage which was to become increasingly important in the celebration of marriage between Christians.[7]

A similar development seems to have taken place in regard to the anointing of the sick. Given a specific human situation, namely, a crisis involving the continuance or the quality of life, the Church took advantage of the sacramental symbolic outlook to read this human situation through the eyes of faith. It realized that sickness has a significance, a fullness of meaning, that goes beyond appearances. It was then that the Church developed a liturgy centered around the oil blessed by the bishop and having for its purpose to proclaim to Christians a message of liberation and hope. The Church wanted to reveal to Christians, amid the painful experience of illness, a God who was calling them to life and giving a new meaning to their sufferings and possible death by bringing them to share the eschatological expectation.

The Church did not apply this sacramental outlook only to Christians who were entering marriage or who had fallen ill. History shows us the Church making use of it to interpret the various situations and events in the life of the Christian. It was in this perspective that people looked, for example, at the ceremony of the anointing of kings or religious profession, as well as at the numerous objects used in Christian worship; a St. Augustine could therefore legitimately refer to numerous *sacramenta*.

With the help of this outlook, the Church was able to understand better its own sacramental nature and its vocation with regard to the sacraments. This is what explains the ambiguities and tortuous history of the Christian rites and of what since the Middle Ages have been called the sacramentals. It also explains the Church's many hesitations about this or that event in the life of Christians as having a sacramental value. This is the case, for example, with Christian marriage.

Given this history, we must pose the question of the origin and institution of the Church's seven sacraments in a new and quite different way. In our view, it is impossible by the historical method to trace each and all of the seven sacraments back to Christ. But if we take a theological approach to the question, that is, if

---

7. See Schillebeeckx, *Marriage*; Rey-Mermet, *Ce que Dieu a uni.*

we see the seven sacraments of the Church as prolongations of the sacramentality of Christ and his Church, then we necessarily see them as related to Christ. At the same time, Christ becomes much more than a simple inventor or institutor of the sacraments; he becomes, as it were, the foundation for every sacramental action because it is through these actions that he acts as a sacrament toward the men of every generation.

In this question of institution, then, it is appropriate to distinguish two different approaches: according to the one, Christ performed certain specific acts of institution; according to the other, he revealed to his apostles, by certain words and actions, that henceforth they were to be the Church, that is, the sacrament of himself. In the Church's thinking at an earlier time, attention was focused on the former approach. This was understandable, given the rejection of the sacramental septenary by the Reformers. It was necessary to prove at any cost that Christ had instituted the seven sacraments. We know the exegetical acrobatics the authors of the theological manuals had to perform in order to support their assertions.

Without rejecting this first approach, theologians today are attaching greater importance to the second. It is more important to bring to light the convictions and thinking that inspired the first Christian communities as they shared the Lord's Supper, performed baptisms, and reflected on the services which the Church had organized for itself than it is to look for the precise moment when Jesus instituted this or that sacrament and for the exact words by which he did it. The use to be made of Scripture then becomes quite different.

All this leads us to broaden the notion of the institution of the sacraments; to situate the classical thesis on institution in a wider context—that of the meaning of certain actions of Christ and his disciples; and finally to correct the excessively materialistic and juridical mentality that seeks to obtain for each sacrament a reference to a word or action of Christ or a determination by him of this or that sacramental matter and form.

Such an enlargement of concepts and approach enables us to give a different meaning to the classical thesis on institution and to discover that certain actions, such as the Last Supper, had a special value in Christ's eyes, that is, had a fullness of meaning which made it more than a simple meal. The same holds for the first Christian communities, which quickly became aware of the sacramental dimension of certain services, certain activities, or certain persons. This is the case with the Lord's Supper,[8] services to the community, and even persons, all of these being viewed in a theological perspective as gifts of the Lord to his Church. When St. Paul condemns those who are at odds because of their allegiances to the various individuals who had baptized them, he makes the Christian sacramental symbolism explicit by telling them that the minister is of little importance, since it is Christ who baptizes.[9]

The important thing to keep in mind here is that Christ is not the institutor of the sacraments in the juridical sense of the term. He is something more than that: he is the foundation of every sacramental reality. This means that his presence is not restricted to a specific act of institution but is necessary for the very existence of any and every sacramental reality.

The history of sacramental practice in the Church also explains the diversity of the sacraments. We can ask: Why seven sacraments? Why several? Strictly speaking, two would have been enough: baptism and the Eucharist. In saying this, we are not far from what was the actual situation in the first centuries of the Church's life when people spoke only of the sacraments of Christian initiation and the Eucharist. Other sacramental actions were very rare and not clearly identified. The Church quickly became aware, however, that man's life provided it with other choice occasions for exercising its vocation of being a sacrament, a vocation that really could not be limited to only a few actions. The Church finally settled on seven such actions; taken symbolically, the number seven meant that the whole of human life is open to the whole of the paschal mystery.[10]

From God's point of view, his presence is always one and the same, but it is conditioned by the situation in the life of the individual or the community. It is the same with the sacraments as with our human encounters. When we meet people, it is the same personal subjects—ourselves—who meet others, and yet we observe that our presence is not of the same kind when we meet a friend in trouble as when we meet the same friend and he is bubbling over with joy. What happens? The mode of our presence is altered by the state of the other person.

---

8. 1 Cor. 11:17–34.
9. 1 Cor. 1:10–16.
10. See Jacques Dournes, "Why Are There Seven Sacraments?" in E. Schillebeeckx and B. Willems (eds.), *The Sacraments in General* (Concilium 31; New York, 1967), pp. 67–86.

The same is true in the sacraments. It is always the same God who is present to us, but when the person is experiencing conflict, God presents himself to him as reconciler and bringer of peace; when the person is experiencing love, it is the face of the God who is Love that the Church shows him; when the person sees his life threatened, it is the God of hope and life that the Church shows him. This means that the diversity of the sacraments is not to be explained in terms of God, since it is always the same God who is present to man. The diversity is required therefore by the condition of man, who craves to see the face of God from various angles, as it were; besides, God cannot reveal himself completely to man in any one sacramental action.

*The utilization of the principles of symbolism
in classical sacramental theology
and in the new effort at sacramental systematization*

Christian sacramental symbolism has a place in every attempt to systematize sacramental theology. We find it in St. Augustine and St. Thomas under the rubric of sign.

St. Augustine describes a sacrament as the sign of a sacred reality (*signum rei sacrae*).[11] He was to be followed by a number of medieval theologians, such as Lanfranc and Hugh of St. Victor. The definition is not very specific and leaves room for a number of interpretations. Nonetheless, St. Augustine did grasp the principle underlying the sacraments, since he defined a sacrament by using the concept of sign; a sign refers man to a further reality that is signified by the first and more readily perceptible reality.

After the later theologians had groped their way, St. Thomas, despite early hesitations of his own, did not find any better category than sign to account for the sacraments. It would be interesting to follow Thomas' development from the *Commentary on the Sentences* to the *Summa*. We would find him wavering on two points: on the category in which the sacraments are to be placed, and on the integration of the two aspects, signification and causality, of the sacraments. St. Thomas' merit is that he defined the sacraments in terms of meaning, thus expressing the two principles of Christian sacramental symbolism. In reasserting the connection of sacrament with sign, he was forced to provide clarifications. In his day, the problem was to qualify the Augustinian idea that

---

11. *De civitate Dei* X, 5; cited in St. Thomas, *Summa theologiae* III, q. 60, a. 1, sed contra, and a. 2, sed contra.

everything is a sacrament. St. Thomas did this, with a good deal of caution, by asserting that a sacrament in the narrower sense causes by signifying or causes in accordance with its power to signify.

The important thing in all this is that these theologians realized that a sacrament has meaning only insofar as it refers to another reality. By that very fact they accepted the principles according to which, first, man has the ability to grasp the symbolic dimension of persons and events, and, second, these persons and events can signify something more than they manifest at first sight.

Quite recently, contemporary theologians have been attempting new syntheses of sacramental theology by taking as their point of departure key ideas other than sign. E. Schillebeeckx, for example, calls upon the more personalist and existential notion of *encounter*, which has the concept of relation for its philosophical context.[12] R. Didier attempts a different synthesis based on the idea of the *word*.[13]

In applying the idea of encounter to the sacraments Father Schillebeeckx has taken sacramental symbolism fully into account. For encounter is a rich and complex concept that embraces a number of interpersonal factors. To begin with, encounter presupposes an invitation or initiative from one of the two parties; it also presupposes an attitude of welcome and receptivity on both sides and has as its result a revelation of each party to himself and to the other. After a genuine encounter we see the other differently than before, but we also see ourselves differently. Finally, a genuine encounter calls for a transformation of the self, a different manner of acting, a new commitment. This is evident in the encounter of a pair of lovers. Their lives are transformed. They have a new reason for living.

All these factors are also to be found in the sacramental encounter. God takes the initiative and comes to meet man in the latter's own situation. He reveals himself to man and reveals man to himself. Moreover, a transformation takes place. Just as a person is no longer the same after a genuine encounter, so the human person is no longer the same after a real encounter with God in a sacrament.

The thinking of Father Didier, who takes the word as his point of reference, leads to a like result. "Word" must, of course, be

---

12. **Schillebeeckx,** *Christ the Sacrament of the Encounter with God.*
13. *L'Eucharistie, le sens des sacrements* (Lyons, 1971), pp. 166–71, 300–14.

given its fullest density of meaning, so that it includes the meaning of the biblical *dabar*.[14] The word in this context is perceived to be an expression of the person. It does more than convey an intellectual message; rather, it is the person himself achieving a new form of an expression. As a result, the word produces the same effect as the presence of the person does. Thus, while undoubtedly revealing the person, it does something more: it challenges, it "dynamizes," it transforms the one who receives it. This explains why St. John could describe Jesus as the "Word of God."

Behind these various presentations of the sacraments we always find the same sacramental symbolism. It is important to keep this symbolism in mind, for it helps us perceive what a sacrament really is. It is always in the background of the various theological formulations, whether they build on the concept of sign or the concept of encounter or the concept of word.

2 — The "Actants" in Sacramental Symbolic Activity

In Christian sacramental symbolism, three principal actants play a role: the Church, man (represented by an individual), and Christ. It is important to establish the role of each as well as the relations between them, because any mistake in interpreting the articulation and connection of the three gives rise to theological distortions and inadequate pastoral methods.

Classical sacramental theology stated indeed that for a sacrament certain conditions were required on the part of the individual. We may ask, however, to what extent the effort was made to assure these conditions. Were they not in fact simplified and thus minimized, especially those having to do with the Church, to the point that once the rite was performed by a validly ordained minister and in the manner that the preoccupation with ritual required, there was no further thought given to the influence and role of the Church in sacramental activity? A major factor in the present renewal is that the sacraments are now located by reference to three roles: the Church, man, and Christ. In fact, the movement of renewal has not only related the sacramental action to these three reference points; it has also indicated how their three roles are to be articulated in practice.

The Church

By describing the Church in sacramental terms, Vatican II gave

---

14. On this subject see André Feuillet and Pierre Grelot, "Word of God," in Léon-Dufour (ed.), *Dictionary of Biblical Theology*, pp. 666–70.

it a new place in the universe of the sacraments and made it the primary point of reference for all sacramental activity. This represents a change of perspective, and theologians and pastors have not yet explored all the avenues it opens up. Nevertheless, everyone is happy to emphasize the communal and ecclesial aspect of every sacramental action. The revised rituals also give evidence of the theological progress in this area.

This aspect of the contemporary renewal of sacramental theology is important enough that we should make an effort to realize the consequences it entails. But we can ask whether pastors in their current approach to the sacraments have really seen clearly the implications of this renewal. There is reason to think that despite their efforts to promote sacramental celebrations in which the community is involved, pastors are too readily satisfied with simply juxtaposing a number of actions by individuals. And yet the integration into the sacramental rite of the Church as principal agent has important consequences. As we saw in recalling how the Fathers thought in this matter, the Church is not only the place of the community's celebration but the principal actor in it. This means that the Church has an inalienable role to play in a sacramental action; it is a beneficiary of the grace of the sacrament by the same title as the individual is.

We think it advisable to make clear the meaning of "Church" in this context. "Church" here means first and foremost the concrete ecclesial community composed of individuals; no part of this community is excluded. It comprises parents, friends, pastoral team, priest, etc. This local Church is made up of various groups of Christians; it is thus something very concrete. No question here of an abstract, distant Church! The Church that is a sacrament is a Church that is very close to the individual, a Church that speaks to him with all the wealth of meaning attaching to the sign which it is, but also with the ambiguity attaching to this same sign.

Having thus defined "Church," we must now assert that this Church is the point of departure of a sacramental action. This statement says something new, and it is essential that we underscore it. In the past we experienced a sacrament as something involving only the individual; this is a perspective we must change. It is the Church that is the point of departure for the entire pastoral sacramental ministry, because it is the Church that gives concrete presence and effectiveness to God's initiative, which is an important factor in the Church's own vocation as a sacrament. This vocation is something that has to be rediscovered, now that the Church no longer lives in a Christian society. In a Christian society, people naturally went to the Church to ask for the rites of baptism, marriage, and so forth. In the new kind of society in which we are now living, people are less inclined to seek the sacraments. They experience the situations of their life without relating them to the Church. Here is where the Church becomes an issue. It is here that the Church's role is changing.

There is no reason to be surprised that people have little or no grasp of the meaning provided by a Christian experience of this or that situation of life and that they do not always feel the need of it. The Church must therefore become more aware of the service it has to offer, a service that will require of it a new consciousness and new ways of acting. The community must accept its responsibility and see to it that people acquire a right understanding, based on faith, of life and its happenings. The community must bear in mind that in its pastoral administration of the sacraments it concretizes God's initiative and brings it to bear on a particular individual so as to raise him up into a new realm of meaning to which he does not naturally have access. Such an undertaking requires a new kind of pastoral practice.

It is easy to discern a mistaken tendency in contemporary pastoral practice regarding the sacraments. Some pastors, impelled by the desire not to distort the truth of the sacraments, are making greater demands on those who request baptism for their child and on young couples who ask for a blessing on their marital union. After inquiring into the quality of the faith of these individuals, pastors may advise against the sacrament. This is a very unfortunate kind of pastoral practice in regard to the sacraments; we might label it a pastoral practice of selectivity, a sieve-in-hand pastoral practice. In it the pastor's role is to sort out those who have sufficient knowledge and will submit to conditions set down by a type of Christianity that is often enough reducible to the practice of Sunday Mass. And yet, once we set aside the traditional criterion of Sunday practice, it becomes quite difficult to evaluate a person's faith!

If we analyze this kind of pastoral practice theologically, we see that it bears the impress of a sacramental theology which does not start with the Church as principal actor or point of reference. It starts with the individual and requires him to have a clear grasp of the meaning of his state of life. This kind of pastoral practice arose within a Church that pursued its tranquil way in the context of Christendom. But that context has changed. We now live in a pluralist, neutral, and even indifferent society. The Church is therefore obliged to revise its position; it can no longer think of itself as having a monopoly on spiritual goods which it distributes to those it thinks worthy. It must rather present itself as a sacrament, that is, as sign and instrument of salvation.[15] In other words, it must offer itself as the means whereby people can acquire the new vision of their life or their situation which Christian experience alone can provide.

Furthermore, in the inadequate kind of pastoral practice we are discussing, there is at work a conception of the sacrament as coextensive in practice with the rite and celebration as such. Where the new ecclesial approach to the sacraments is lacking, pastors are too often satisfied with juxtaposing a series of individualistically conceived actions and giving people the impression of a Church which is fussy and intransigent. The Church is there only in order to sort people out!

Is this to say that the Church should not be selective at all but should accept into its sacramental celebrations people who do not enter into the spirit of the Church's sacramental symbolism? By no means! In certain cases the Church must make a prudential judgment. But there is need of determining the criteria by which it is to make this judgment. Until now the tendency has been to judge the faith of the individuals who ask for the sacrament. But everyone knows that it is extremely difficult to assess someone's faith; in consequence this practice is often misunderstood. Would it not be possible instead to make a selection on the basis of different kinds of expression of faith and different kinds of relation to the Church? How can someone cooperate in an action of the Church if he is not truly a member of the Church? In addition, should not the other aspects of sacramentality, namely, a sacrament's functions and dimensions, be made a criterion for selection?

In summary, it can be said that the awareness of the Church as agent in the sacramental action is of primary importance in the current liturgical renewal and in the efforts being made by the Churches to find themselves in today's world. All this is based on the theological principle that the Church "sacramentalizes" God's initiatives in regard to mankind.

This shift of emphasis from the sacramental rite to the Church

---

15. See the conciliar Constitution on the Church, no. 1.

as sacrament raises new problems, since it expands the framework of sacramentality and allows a certain ambiguity to persist. It may be asked, for example, what connection there is between the overall pastoral sacramental activity of the Church and the pastoral action of the Church which accompanies one or other of the seven sacraments.

This situation which the new ecclesiology has brought about also has its advantages. It does involve a certain ambiguity, but the use of this kind of terminology has the advantage, on the one hand, of highlighting the sacramental nature of every action of the Church (here we are in clear continuity with Vatican II) and, on the other, of making it clear that all of life, and not just the moment of the celebration of a sacrament, is sacramental. In addition to bringing out the fact that the Church is sacramental in all its activity, this new vocabulary shows that the Church gives a privileged place to certain situations and actions in which it fulfills in a special way its vocation to be a sacrament, even though its sacramental action continues to embrace more than the seven sacraments.

It is of interest here to note that even in the most classical sacramental theology, which defended the thesis that the sacraments are seven in number, no more and no fewer,[16] there was an awareness that the Church's vocation to be a sacrament could not be limited to these seven privileged actions. It was at a time when the idea of seven sacraments took root that the term "sacramentals" became part of the theologian's vocabulary. This was because people had soon become aware that other gestures or actions of the Church shared more or less fully in its sacramental nature.

Admittedly, our new situation will cause problems, since people have become accustomed only to seven quite specific actions as sacraments. But these problems will undoubtedly seem secondary as compared with the undeniable advantages of a more comprehensive outlook on the sacramental world. The new approach will educate Christians to a better grasp of the Church's sacramental dimension, a point strongly emphasized by Vatican II in its new ecclesiology. In addition, this new vision will make it possible to integrate the sacraments into the general pastoral practice of the Church instead of isolating them and fostering a distinction between a pastoral approach to the sacraments, a pas-

---

16. See G. Dumeige's collection of conciliar pronouncements, *La foi catholique* (Paris, 1969), no. 663 (extracts from the Council of Trent).

toral approach to evangelization, and so on. Properly understood, the broader concept of sacrament can only be advantageous to the Church and to the sacraments themselves, since the latter will acquire once again the fullness of meaning they should have in the life of the Church and the Christian.

The emphasis on the Church as an "actant" in sacramental symbolism suggests two reminders. First, the sacraments should not be thought of in the restrictive context of a single minister and a single believer. Second, the efficacy and signification of a sacrament should not be looked at solely from the viewpoint of the subject of the celebration. As an agent and not simply as the place of, or witness to, the sacrament, the Church is the recipient of grace and meaning by the same title as the individual who takes the personal sacramental step. This point is fundamental to an understanding of the fuller meaning of the community that undertakes a sacramental celebration, in particular communal celebrations of forgiveness.

Man

It is unnecessary to attempt to prove the importance of the personal or individual aspect of an ecclesial sacramental action. The point is evident and denied by no one. As a matter of fact, the renewal of sacramental theology is giving it an increased importance. The Constitution on the Liturgy and the revised rituals are very explicit on this point. The real novelty is that importance is being attached once again not only to man in general but to the concrete individual acting in a concrete situation. For, as we have seen, salvation embraces the individual in his existential totality.

Traditional theology liked to repeat the adage: "The sacraments are for the sake of man." Nothing could be truer. But it must be admitted that the inflexibility of ritualism, aggravated by the inflexibility of an exaggerated rubricism, prevented the full application of this classical adage. And yet it was not always so in the sacramental practice of the Church. The first appearance of rituals in the work of Hippolytus of Rome has a good deal to say to us on this subject.[17] Hippolytus undoubtedly had no intention of imposing a single immutable way of celebrating sacramentally some situation of human life. His intention was rather to offer

---

17. The *Apostolic Tradition* is the first collection of rituals that has survived; most of the items in it are attributed to Hippolytus of Rome.

a model for various celebrations. However, as everyone knows, the idea of the ritual as model later gave way to the ritual as a fixed framework, a narrow track from which it was not permitted to depart.

For all that, the practice of the Church did make room for flexibility and creativity. It is interesting to observe that in the disciplinary decrees of the Council of Trent—the Council to which all the deviations in theology and in the life of the Church in recent centuries have been wrongly attributed—a great deal of leeway is allowed for catechetical explanation within the very celebration of the sacred mysteries. Even though the Fathers of the Council of Trent retained the use of Latin in the liturgy, they were aware of the difficulty this practice entailed. It was on this account that they called for the explanation, in the vernacular, of the rites and of the meaning of the mysteries being celebrated, and this during the celebration itself. Unfortunately this point escaped the attention of pastors and theologians. The latter were for the most part content to follow the ritual with scrupulous fidelity.

In practice there was nevertheless a certain flexibility at the level of the local Churches. For example, we find priests composing Masses and having them approved by the bishop. This was the case especially with St. John Eudes, who composed Masses in honor of the Sacred Hearts of Jesus and Mary; they were approved by the bishops of several dioceses such as Rennes, Coutances, Evreux, Rouen, and finally by Bishop de Laval in 1662.[18]

The campaign to romanize the liturgy during the nineteenth century, especially starting with Dom Guéranger, led to a uniformity that was not very compatible with the principle that "the sacraments are for the sake of man." Vatican II realized this and opened the door to adaptation, flexibility, and creativity, as is evident from the new rituals and the liturgical Constitution. At this point we may ask to what extent the Churches have taken advantage of these new possibilities of adaptation and creativity (which are not to be confused with spontaneity and improvisation). We can also ask to what extent people know how to use the rituals. Did they simply replace one ritual with another on a certain day, or have they been able to see in the recent official books a new pedagogical, liturgical, and theological aid in living sacramentally the various situations of life? For if the goal intended is to be at-

18. St. John Eudes, *Oeuvres complètes* 7:350–67; 8:379.

tained, namely, to emphasize the role of man and the situations of his life, then the revision of the rituals must be accompanied by a new mentality and a new approach to the rituals themselves.

The focusing of attention on the person as seen in his concrete situation creates a problem when we endeavor to relate this focus to the Church. The question arises of how to relate the step being taken by an individual to the action of the community, since the latter is important by the same title as the individual. The problem is serious at the pastoral level and the theological level alike. Which action is to be given primacy: that of the individual or that of the Church? How are the two to be articulated?

These questions are not new ones. They are connected with the larger and more comprehensive theological problem of the relation between God's prevenient action or initiative and man's response. In this matter a few points are certain. For one thing, two factors must be respected: the initiative of God and the response of man, even if we do not see with full clarity the inner relationship of the two. In addition, we must reaffirm that God comes first in the sacramental process and that man's activity is always a response to this initiative. The sacraments should therefore call attention to both aspects. They should symbolize the fact that God takes the initiative in making himself known to man on the occasion of a particular event in the latter's life, and they should also render visible the assent or response of man to this initiative.

If we put too much emphasis on man's role and his assent, we veil the fact that God really has the initiative in a sacrament, and we frequently leave the impression that man earns or buys his salvation at the cost of satisfying certain conditions. On the other hand, an exclusive emphasis on the initiative that God exercises via the community leaves the impression of a certain passivity on man's part. An inadequate integration of these two aspects falsifies the problem of infant baptism and of the anointing of a sick person who is unconscious. It is therefore very important to articulate properly the two dimensions, God's initiative and man's response, and never to separate them.

In practice, a sacramental action by the community cannot exist unless the persons involved enter into it and carry it out together. The question here is how the personal commitment of faith and the activity of the community are to be integrated with one another. In a sacrament, personal assent must be articulated with the action of Christ and the action of the Church. In fact, a sacrament is even the privileged locus for the proper integration of all three. In the world of the sacraments we cannot regard God's intervention, the Church's activity, and man's involvement as mutually antagonistic. The three are harmoniously interwoven. The attempt has often been made, it is true, to safeguard the action of Christ in the sacraments by minimizing the active role of man. But the attempt is a misguided one, since the divine intervention takes place through the medium of man's action: not solely the action of a minister or a community but also the action of the recipient, who takes an active part in the process. Personal assent combines with that of the Church to render visible the action of Christ.

These reflections on man as agent in the sacramental process suggest four remarks on pastoral practice.

1. The sacramental process should take advantage of the individual's experience. It is with a human situation such as life, conflict, love, sickness or death as its starting point that the Church is to proclaim the fullness of meaning which the message of Christ bestows.

2. It is good to recall that the individual, if left to his own resources, is unable to discover the full meaning of his situation. He doubtless raises certain questions to start with, but we must remember that it is God who takes the initiative by entering the person's life in order to lead him beyond his first interpretation of his own experience and open up to him a realm of meaning which only God can disclose to man.

3. In view of the inevitable tension between God's initiative and man's personal response, let us recall that no single celebration of a given sacrament can enable a person to experience all the dimensions of its meaning in the same degree. Thus sometimes the celebration of a baptism will give a better insight into God's initiative (this is the typical result in the case of infant baptism); at other times it will accentuate man's personal response (this is more readily the case in adult baptism). Something similar holds for the other kinds of sacramental activity.

4. Finally, attention to the three points of reference for every sacrament—Christ, the Church, and man—leads us to broaden our idea of signification or efficacy. If the Church is truly a principal "actant" in the sacramental process, it is also a beneficiary of it, so that the efficacy of the sacrament is not to be measured solely

in terms of the subject who "receives the sacrament." The community itself, as participant in the celebration and not a mere spectator at a rite involving only the minister and the recipient, also shares in the grace which the sacrament effects. This is a point that seems to be lost from sight in the pastoral approach to the sacraments.

Christ

In the sacramental process, the activity of man and especially the activity of the Church should not absorb our whole attention. They should rather lead us on to another actant: Christ. In the last analysis, he is the one most fully active in a sacrament.

We said at the beginning of Chapter 2 that Christ is the great sacrament of the Father and that he is even, in St. Augustine's phrase, the only sacrament of God. We should not lose sight of that statement as we reflect on the sacraments of the Church. In the sacramental order, Christ remains the great sacrament. He must be taken into account as we endeavor to understand the Christian sacramental rites; otherwise we risk losing any truly sacramental perspective even in dealing with the sacraments.

It is interesting to find that this intuition is at work in a number of theses in classical sacramental theology. It is at the basis of the thinking on the minister of the sacraments[19] and on the efficacy of the sacraments.[20] It is clear indeed that the role of Christ is not isolated from all else, for it is linked to the role of the Church which concretizes it. But we must not lose sight of it, for if we do, we are in danger of giving the sacramental process the appearance of something magical; we run the risk of attributing to a rite the grace which Christ alone can effect. As St. Thomas says, "It is evident that in a special way the sacraments of the Church derive their power from the passion of Christ."[21] And he adds: "It is necessary therefore that saving power should flow from the divinity of Christ through his humanity into the sacraments."[22]

Fortunately, current sacramental theology is emphasizing the fact that a sacrament prolongs the action of Christ who is rendered visible by the Church. How are we to describe this action

---

19. St. Thomas, *Summa theologiae* III, q. 64, aa. 1 and 3.

20. *Ibid.*, III, q. 62, a. 5c.

21. *Ibid.*: "Manifestum est quod sacramenta Ecclesiae specialiter habent virtutem ex passione Christi."

22. *Ibid.*: "Et ideo oportet quod virtus salutifera derivatur a divinitate Christi per eius humanitatem in ipsa sacramenta."

of Christ? The great theologians, St. Thomas among them, are not very explicit on this point. On the subject of Christ's action in the sacraments, St. Thomas speaks of "the mysterious power of Christ" but does not explain further. If we are to understand in some measure this sacramental activity of Christ, we must first look at his activity as a whole. In all the situations of our life we are called to live in union with Christ. Father Traets writes that

> in all situations and at every moment of our life the glorified Christ makes us share his own life and destiny. He makes this life present and operative in us in order that we may live as he lived and as he continues to live now: with him, in him, through him. Therefore we may not limit the actualization in us of Christ's life solely to the moments of sacramental celebration.[23]

Christ acts, first of all, through his Spirit who is present in the world dispensing life, love, joy, peace, and truth, giving hope to the despairing, and stimulating creativity. Christ becomes present in a special way through his word as proclaimed and lived in various manners. The reference here is certainly to the word as proclaimed in a liturgical context, but also to the word as embodied in the lives of Christians. Christ also speaks through his Church, that is, through all the Christians who manifest his presence and are in a sense his sacrament. He manifests himself, too, through ritual actions which, because they are integrated into the action of faith, become capable of revealing the presence of Christ's saving action in us.

We must emphasize here that in no sacramental action may the rites be regarded in isolation from Christ and the Church. Thus it would be misleading to claim that the bread and wine of the Eucharist are transformed simply on the grounds that Christ's power is present in the sacrament, without at the same time relating this power to the other factors in the sacramental action, namely the Church, the individual, and even the rite. In other words, the power of Christ at work in the sacrament should be articulated with the other two actants of the sacrament: the Church and man himself. We can conclude from this that in any sacramental action it is not the ritual components as such that are the most important factor but the persons who make use of them.

We may ask at this point just when the action of Christ is sacramental. Certainly it is such in a special way in the sacramental celebrations of the Church. This point has never been in question. But we are now confronted with something new, since the concept

---

23. "Orientations pour une théologie des sacrements," p. 109.

of sacramentality has been broadened. In the process it has also become more flexible, more comprehensive,[24] and therefore less unequivocal. Today the term "sacrament" is both richer and more ambiguous. The question therefore arises as to what belongs in the universe of sacrament and what does not. Or, more specifically: What is a sacrament and what is not a sacrament? In a sense, every activity of Christ is sacramental. God has always acted through intermediaries. The author of the Letter to the Hebrews says as much in his prologue: "In many and various ways God spoke of old to our fathers through the prophets; but in these last days he has spoken to us by a Son."[25]

God has always revealed himself by means of signs which both manifest and hide his presence. The glorified Christ is no exception to this rule. He makes himself visible, perceptible, by means of signs. In the present economy of salvation, therefore, we are surrounded by many signs of the presence and activities of Christ, signs which represent various degrees of Christian sacramental symbolism. This means we live in a sacramental universe whose contours are much less clear-cut than in the past, but it is also a universe that is much richer and more inclusive. What we have lost in clarity and definiteness, we have gained in richness of meaning.

3 — The Functions of Sacramental Symbolism

If we take as our starting point the sacramentality of Christ, and in particular the functions he exercises insofar as he is sacrament, we can specify another aspect of sacramental symbolism with the help of the category of function. Christ spoke about his Father, made him known, and showed that he himself was the actualization of the Father's presence. "He who sees me sees the Father," St. John tells us.

The Church as sacrament of Christ also exercises specific functions: it reveals the Father, the Son, and the Spirit; it embodies their presence; and it reveals the meaning of man. Classical sacramental theology had a good deal to say about sacramental efficacy and thus focused attention on a particular function of the sacramental process, namely, the function of making actual or real. The other functions were there but were perhaps neglected during

---

24. "Comprehensive" is understood here according to the etymology of the word: it embraces a wider range of things.

25. Heb. 1:1–2.

certain periods of the Church's life.

If we let ourselves be guided by the current liturgical renewal and the thinking it has stimulated, as well as by the lessons of history, we can say that the Church's sacramental action has three very specific functions: proclamation or revelation, realization or actualization, and finally celebration. With the aid of these functional categories, we shall endeavor to understand the sacramental activity of the Church, man, and Christ in its existential aspect. They will provide us with a framework in which to locate a number of theses from classical sacramental theology and to reincorporate a number of essential questions that were left aside during the second phase of sacramental theology and the sacramental life.

Revelation

The writings of the Church Fathers who describe the sacramental practice of the early centuries attribute great importance to proclamation or revelation as a dynamic factor in the sacramental process. The ecclesial communities of the time were very conscious of their vocation and wanted to reveal to Christians the many aspects of the mystery of salvation. They did so in sacramental celebrations which, in the case of Christian initiation, were spread out over many weeks. At the various stages of human life, the communities helped their members to discover facets of God as well as the full meaning available to the human person in a given situation of his life.

This function of the sacraments ceased to be a primary concern once the Church had taken root in the Western world and was less preoccupied with revealing its own mystery than with showing the moral implications of a mystery with which Christians were assumed to be already familiar. In this phase of the Church's life, from the Middle Ages to our own day, emphasis was put on another function of the sacraments: making actual or real.

All was not smooth sailing, however, In fact, the neglect of the dynamic factor of proclamation was an important cause of the reaction of the Reformers. As is well known, the Reformers aggressively deplored the absence of the revealing word from the sacraments; in popular practice the sacraments were very much open to a magical interpretation. The Reformers rediscovered the role of the word but were unable to articulate it fully with the ritual aspect.

This led to two conceptions of the Church's life: that of the Reformers, which would be summed up as "the Church of the word," and that of the Roman Catholic Church, which would be described as "the Church of the sacraments." It is clear that these views of the Church and sacramentality held the field down to our own day. The choice between a pastoral practice focused on the sacraments and a pastoral practice focused on evangelization arose because ecclesiology and sacramentality were not integrated.

In other words, the context in which this choice arose was the same context that produced the Reformation. Observing that many Christians were still practicing but had little knowledge of God's word, those in the pastoral ministry said: "The time is past for a pastoral practice focused on the sacraments; the need now is for a pastoral practice focused on evangelization." This problem received no response at the time when it was raised, but it surfaced again when the Church became aware that it was no longer coextensive with the world around it and that its believing members had little understanding of what a sacrament really meant. This awareness arose in academic circles and among pastors who had to deal with young couples at the time of their marriage and of their child's baptism. But behind the problem lay a false conception of the sacraments. If the problem was raised in those terms, it was because pastors were approaching the sacraments in a way that left little room for the word within the sacramental process. Was that how Christian tradition had understood the sacraments? What does Vatican II have to say on the subject?

At the practical level, the sacramental renewal of Vatican II accorded an unequivocal place to the word. The Constitution on the Liturgy sets down the principles in this matter,[26] while the new rituals emphasize the word by introducing a liturgy of the word into every celebration of a sacrament, even the private celebration of reconciliation. The new practice is not inspired by an apologetic purpose, but expresses the new conception of sacramentality of which Vatican II had become aware. It is a conception that answers the question which the Reformers were putting to the Church of their day. One of the most important aspects of the renewal of sacramental theology by Vatican II is that the Council joined word and sacrament, so that a sacrament no longer gives the impression of being exclusively a rite that produces something.

---

26. Nos. 24 and 35.

Several factors evidently played a part in giving a place of honor to the word in the sacramental life: the study of the sources and a better knowledge of the history of sacramental practice, but also a consciousness that Christians are becoming a minority. The overall context, too, is entirely new. For the first time in its history, the Church is being forced to live and proclaim the mystery of Christ in a world that is areligious, at least in outward manifestation.

The preaching of the primitive Church, on the other hand, as well as the preaching of the Church during the great periods of missionary activity, was directed to a world in which natural religion was a major factor in life. This is no longer the case. The sacramental life has been profoundly affected in the process; it is changing its function. It is no longer being viewed as a form of worship that is owed to God, but as a sign of membership in a social group which is differentiated from the bulk of mankind. A sacramental celebration must have as one of its functions to render explicit the purposes that motivate its participants and make them different from others. The pastoral approach to the sacraments must foster an awareness of the specific meaning attached to Christian life.

This new state of affairs has not yet become general in our milieu, but it can be seen approaching; without making any pessimistic forecast about the future of Church and society, it is evident that the new situation will become more and more the rule. This, then, is the specific context in which the sacramental life is to be lived. We can therefore understand better the emphasis that must be put on the role of revelation in the pastoral approach to the sacraments.

We may ask, however, to what extent this conception of the relation between word and sacrament is in continuity with Christian tradition. The studies which induced the Fathers of the Council to describe the Church as the sacrament of salvation have also made possible a better grasp of the origins and history of our word "sacrament" and of the reality it has designated in the course of the centuries. The origins of the word are indeed obscure, but it is certainly related to the Greek *mysterion* of St. Paul, for whom the term signifies the secret plan of God as revealed by his Son, the man Jesus. This unique *mysterion* was prefigured in the old covenant and is experienced in Christian liturgical celebrations. In the latter case the Fathers spoke of *mysteria* (the plural of *mysterion*).

The Latin translation of the Bible went and hunted out the word *sacramentum* as a designation for the mysteries celebrated in Christian worship. But this does not mean that our word "sacrament" can signify only liturgical rites. It does refer to these, but only to the extent that they reveal, make real, and celebrate the events that wrought our salvation in Jesus Christ. In other words, in the original use of our word "sacrament," the aspect of manifestation, revelation, or epiphany took priority over the aspect of instrumentality, rite, and causality. In his book *Un peuple messianique*,[27] Father Congar has a fine summary of the work done on the history of the word *sacramentum* and of its relations with the corresponding Greek word *mysterion*. He ends his summary as follows:

> We may therefore assert that the role of the word in the sacraments is essential. It is essential in respect of the rite itself, according to the well-known statement of St. Augustine that was to be constantly repeated later on: "The word is added to the element, and the result is a sacrament." The words in question are not just any words but words that likewise refer to God's plan of salvation and to the covenant; they are therefore words which act as a memorial that actualizes the saving intervention of God and the mystery (mysteries) of Christ. The words in this case are not simply cognitive, not simply the expression of ideas and sentiments, but are in their own proper way a communication of the reality or actualization of it that reaches its completion in the celebration of this reality.[28]

It is this particular point that the theological renewal associated with Vatican II grasped so well and has brought it to the fore in sacramental theology and especially in the sacramental liturgy. The new rituals are clear proof of this. The Council's teaching was confirmed in some statements of Pope Paul VI. In his Apostolic Exhortation on Evangelization, for example, he wrote:

> Evangelization therefore reveals its full potentiality when it establishes a close link, or rather an unbroken continuity, between word and sacrament. Ambiguity is the result when, as sometimes happens, an opposition is set up between the preaching of the Gospel and the administration of the sacraments. Undeniably, of course, to administer the sacraments without having given solid catechetical instruction on them or even without any general catechesis is to deprive the sacraments in large measure of their effectiveness. The duty of the evangelist is to educate men in the faith so that each Christian will be induced to live the sacraments as authentic sacraments of faith instead of receiving them passively or even unwillingly.[29]

---

27. Chs. 2 and 3.
28. *Ibid.*, p. 53.
29. Apostolic Exhortation *Evangelii nuntiandi*, no. 47, tr. in *The Pope Speaks* 21 (1976), p. 25.

The restored emphasis on the dynamic element of proclamation or revelation, that is, of the word in the understanding of sacramental theology and the sacramental life, suggests three remarks.

1. In the pastoral approach to the sacraments, the revelatory function of the word is twofold. First, it must reveal a facet of God, who, as we said earlier, cannot express himself completely in a single sacramental action. At the pastoral level, it would be appropriate to ask ourselves what aspect of God emerges from this or that sacramental action. What kind of God is revealed by baptism, reconciliation, confirmation, marriage, or the anointing of the sick? This is something we too easily forget about, although it should in fact be an important criterion in developing and evaluating a pastoral approach to the sacraments.

In its other revelatory role, the word must manifest the reality of man as he now is and as he is called to become. If one purpose of the sacraments is to bring to light all the potentialities that in the end will be fully actuated only at the resurrection, then this revelation necessarily has an eschatological dimension. Once again we have here an important point for the pastoral treatment of the sacraments. What image of man does this pastoral approach reveal? Is it defeatist, and does it inculcate guilt? Or does it rouse to action and stimulate?

2. The second remark has to do with the familiar problem of evangelization and sacramentalization. It seems that a sacramental theology which makes the role of the word an integral and essential part of its synthesis will eliminate this false problem according to which we must choose between evangelization and sacramentalization. It is no longer possible to oppose these two activities of the Church. To do so would be to fail to appreciate the riches of sacramental theology; it would be to deprive sacramental theology of a vital factor and thus reduce it to a theory for a rite that simply produces grace. In the name, then, of a complete and rounded sacramental theology, we must abandon this dichotomous view of the Church's activity and regard the proclamation of the word and the celebration of certain actions of the community and individuals as forming a single embodiment of the Church's sacramental activity.

3. If the word is an essential part of a sacramental process, then it may not be regarded as an optional preparation for the sacraments. We may ask here whether the vocabulary we use in

our pastoral practice is in harmony with sacramental theology. We speak much of preparation for the sacraments, meaning something that precedes the sacraments. In other words, we make the sacrament coextensive with the moment of celebration. Admittedly, we do speak of the pastoral approach to the sacraments as including the entire preparation, in which the word plays a large role. But should we not go further and speak simply of the "sacrament" instead of "preparation" for it?

There is a new factor here: the element of time, to which we have not as yet allotted any great importance. It is a factor that makes its appearance, somewhat hesitantly, in the new rituals. In the provisional ritual for adult baptism, time plays an important role, as it did in the liturgy of apostolic times. In the new ritual of penance, too, time is undoubtedly allowed to play a large part. This suggests that we should enlarge our idea of sacrament and not reduce it to the ritual celebration but give it a new comprehension and extension. It is perhaps time, then, for us to remove the word "preparation" (for a sacrament) from our pastoral vocabulary in order to make it clearer that in the preparatory part the pastoral sacramental process is already underway; that the "preparation" is already the sacrament in the early moments of its coming into being through time.

Actualization

The second function of the sacramental process, which we are here calling actualization or realization,[30] follows upon revelation. In a sense, it is simply the unfolding of the revelatory or proclamatory aspect. We saw earlier that the revelatory function of the word included an element of creation or realization (making real), when "word" is understood as equivalent to the *dabar* of the Bible. It is a word that reveals but also a word that creates. Despite the close connection that exists between the function of actualization and the function of revelation, it is preferable to study the two separately, in order to avoid giving the impression that a sacrament has a role to play only in relation to the mind. As a matter of fact, the revelatory function of a sacrament does not consist solely in presenting modern man with a religious message. The message must also be one that leads to a change. It must enter the heart of the believer and be present there like leaven in the dough. Then the individual will receive the word and actualize it

---

30. In this section we shall use the term "actualization."

(make it operative) in his life, so that it will not be a merely intellectual word.

These considerations regarding actualization are not new. Actualization has been the object of reflection, discussion, and opinion among the theologians of every age. In his book on the sacraments,[31] Raymond Didier lists the principal categories theologians have used in their efforts to define and express this particular insight regarding the sacraments. The Fathers of the Church expressed the function of which we are speaking chiefly in terms of *containment* and *identity*. The point of departure for their thinking was the Eucharist, and consequently these terms could be as easily applied to the other sacraments. Nonetheless, this explanation satisfied theologians down to the time of Hugh of St. Victor in the twelfth century.

Peter Lombard then introduced the concept of *cause* to explain the function of realization or creation. From that time on, the concept of cause served to explain this function of a sacrament and gave rise to extended discussions of the causality and efficacy of the sacraments and of their validity and liceity. The important place this whole question had for many centuries in sacramental theology and pastoral practice is well known. In fact, this function drew all the attention of theologians and pastors, so that the other functions of proclamation and celebration became secondary in the Church's mind.

The almost exclusive attention paid by the Church to this particular sacramental function helped to foster a somewhat magical[32] and mechanical view of the causality or efficacy of the sacraments among the Christian people. In addition, the mentality of the Christian people was such that they were inclined to give this function a magical interpretation. We really must not idealize the Christianity of the Middle Ages! The entire people was undoubtedly Christian, but the rite of baptism was not enough to transform the pagan mentality of a whole population. The Christian rites were there, but the people retained a pagan conception of them and a pagan approach to them. In short, pagan rites had been replaced by Christian rites, but the mentality of the people had not changed. This explains why the preachers and theologians of the time paid so much attention to the question of sacramental efficacy.

---

31. *Les sacrements de la foi: La Pâque dans ses signes*, pp. 68–71.
32. The magical conception of the sacraments attributes an almost exclusive value to the rite as such, independently of the actants; as a result, the impression is given that it is the rite, isolated from its ecclesial context, that is efficacious.

What can be said of this question today? To begin with, we must not lay ourselves open to having what we say be given a magical interpretation. We must go even further and endeavor to eradicate this interpretation from the minds of Christians, for it is still alive there. To accomplish this, we must relate the function of actualization to the actants in sacramental symbolic action, namely, Christ, the Church, and man.

By its nature the sacramental rite undoubtedly has a function, and even numerous functions. In the world of sacramental symbolism, these functions are rendered even more specific by relation to the Church, to man, and to Christ, for these three act in the sacramental process. In thinking about this matter, we will do well to refer back to St. Thomas, because he did much to promote accurate thinking about it.

At the beginning of his career as a theologian, St. Thomas was not certain whether he should define a sacrament in terms of sign or in terms of cause. In the *Summa* he makes his choice and defines the sacraments in terms of sign. When, however, he comes to define the efficacy of the sacraments, he falls back on the concept of cause, but does so with important qualifications. He opts for physical causality as opposed to a purely moral or juridical causality. Within the category of physical causality, he chooses instrumental physical causality.[33] Clearly, it is the sacramental rite itself that is being placed in the order of instrumental physical causality.[34] By explaining sacramental efficacy in this way, St. Thomas prevents Christians from yielding to a magical interpretation of it and draws their attention instead to the true and principal cause of a sacrament, namely, the mysterious "power of Christ."

At the same time, however, except for this reference to the power of Christ, St. Thomas' language about sacramental causality is of a negative kind. I do not mean that he had a negative view of this aspect of the sacraments; on the contrary, he locates the sacraments in a perspective that is full of mystery. But since it is difficult

---

33. *Summa theologiae* III, q. 62, a. 1.

34. For the benefit of the reader who is unfamiliar with these categories of scholastic philosophy, we offer a brief explanation. With "physical" cause we are in the realm of the material and the physical. Thus in the building of a house the carpenter is a physical cause; he is even the principal physical cause as compared with his tools, which also belong to the order of physical causes but are instrumental physical causes. When we speak of moral or juridical causality, we enter a different realm. A father who exercises strong authority over his son can be the moral cause of many of his son's actions. A law, too, can be the cause of many positions taken, actions performed, judgments passed, etc.

to express the mystery, he adopts the "negative way," pointing out explanations that are not viable and calling upon the language of causality with its many distinctions. When he attempts to express sacramental causality in positive terms, he has no recourse but to invoke the mysterious power of Christ who acts in and through the Christian rite. Evidently St. Thomas makes no explicit reference in this context to the Church which incarnates and renders visible this mysterious power of Christ. We know now why he does not refer to the Church: it is because in the Middle Ages there was no ecclesiology to accompany sacramental theology.

The mind of St. Thomas saw a close connection between the effect of a sacrament and the meaning of that sacrament. As a result, he has a number of adages or succinctly stated principles which we find repeated by the theologians who came after him and by writers of our own day. Here are some of them: "The sacraments effect what they signify and signify what they effect"; "The sacraments signify grace because they effect it"; "The sacraments effect grace to the extent that they signify it"; "In the sacraments the act of signifying is efficacious"; "The sacraments effect grace according to their power of signifying."

The property that grace has of manifesting itself takes concrete form in the actuality of the Church itself. We understand this better as a result of Vatican II, which stressed the sacramental dimension of the Church. In brief, the relation between the Church and grace is marked by a similar relation between the sacramental sign and the grace it produces. Clearly, it is possible to make this statement only if the Church is linked to grace, that is, manifests grace and makes it real. That may seem to be a vast claim, but in fact the grace-Church relation only states in an explicit way what the reality of "Church" is. There is no such thing as "the Church" apart from the manifestation of grace. Similarly, there is no such thing as "a sacrament" apart from the manifestation of grace.

This theological explanation is not without importance for our discussion of the function of actualization in the sacramental process. The explanation provides us with some principles. The first is negative, but no less important on that account, and has to do with an interpretation of the sacraments that endeavors to steer completely clear of magic. The second is very positive and has to do with the set of factors that come into play in what we are calling "actualization." The rite itself, of course, exercises a number of functions, but it does so only in dependence on the other factors: man, the community, and, of course, Christ. We should bear in mind that the rite does not act by itself, even though it does have a certain natural power to suggest meaning. It functions to the extent that the other three components are operative. Consequently, it acts to the extent that the community, in dependence on Christ, that is, in its essential role as sacrament of Christ, fulfills its function of embodying God's initiative toward man and man's response to God. In addition, there is actualization or sacramental efficacy when an individual accepts the dynamic influence of the word that challenges, stimulates, and transforms. This is what St. Thomas is talking about when he says: "The sacraments effect grace to the extent that they signify it."

It is rather difficult to elucidate this connection between efficacy and signification. Father Traets issues a serious caution in the article which we have already cited:

> At the level of the religious life and therefore of the sacramental life as well, we find ourselves in the presence of a human involvement that is illumined by faith (the active role of the person who expresses himself in a sacramental action); in the process, a saving action (the divine intervention) lays hold of us. It is very important here not to approach the situation with a conceptual scheme that combines these two realities as though they were separate forces whose specific actions we must bring into harmony with the help of some synergizing mechanism. It is even more important not to regard the two as opposed, as if God's action gained in intensity as human participation lessened, or vice versa. We shall be coming back to this point. For the moment we need only point out that in order to understand *the efficacy of the sacraments*, we will do well to take as our starting point the unity of the action we perform and the salvation that comes to us.[35]

The biblical concept of covenant does, however, provide us with a helpful framework. In this context a sacramental efficacy can be seen in the linking of God's call and man's response. In such a context the word plays a prominent role in signifying both God's call and man's answer to it. From this can be seen the importance of the connection which the proclaimed word should have with life. In the covenant there is efficacy to the extent that the signifying word challenges man and influences his life and that of the community—to the extent, that is, that the word is truly accepted. In a sense, the efficacy of the sacrament depends both on the quality of the proclamation made, thanks to symbol and word, and on its reception by the individual and the entire community.

---

35. "Orientations pour une théologie des sacrements," p. 100.

An example may help us understand this aspect of the sacraments. Let us take the case of an anointing of the sick that is celebrated with a person who has been suddenly attacked by serious illness. Let us suppose that a man in his forties, in the prime of life, the father of a family, learns that he has contracted cancer, a disease that inevitably kills. The man has only a few months to live. He cannot understand it. The news fills him with anger and despair. But gradually the Church enters the picture, not as an abstraction but in the form of persons who embody it. His wife, a priest, a friend, or a relative helps him to see his disease, along with his entire life, in the light of hope. The proclamation of the message of hope penetrates his spirit. Slowly the sick man regains hope and a Christian outlook on his disease and his life. Instead of smashing his head against the wall of despair, he finds a way that opens into the future. Gradually he becomes more and more serene, until he ends by accepting his death in the perspective of eschatological expectation and total fulfillment that was invoked upon him at his baptism.

Once this process has taken place, thanks to the sacramental action of a Church made visible in the flesh of men, this Christian, together with Christ and the Church, can now celebrate his pilgrimage of faith at a critical moment in his life. Here we have what can be called the sacramental grace of the anointing of the sick— where "anointing" includes the pastoral approach to the sacrament as well as the rite itself. Is it not a grace (in the sense of unrestricted gift) that this person should find the presence of Christ at a particular moment of his life? The presence becomes a grace because it causes the proclaimed mystery to be effectively operative in human experience. Let us once again emphasize the fact that each sacrament reveals a particular aspect of the Christian mystery by rendering Christ present in this mystery.

The above example will help us understand the meaning of sacramental "actualization." The transformation is the result of the action of Christ, the Church, and the individual himself who has responded to the invitation of Christ as sacramentalized by the Christian community. All these actants have fulfilled the Church's vocation of being a sacrament by their witness and by proclaiming the word of God.

We should not think that the individual—a sick person, a child who is baptized, those who marry—is the only one to benefit from the sacrament. This is a point on which people need to be corrected. In a sacramental theology that left little room for the

Church or the community, the person who "received" the sacrament was in fact the sole beneficiary. Such a theology directed the entire grace effect of the sacrament to the individual. In our view, however, the situation is quite different. In a sacramental theology which restores the community to its true position, making it an actant and not a simple spectator or simply the place of the sacramental action, the community itself is envisaged in the realization or actualization of the sacramental symbolism.

This is strikingly clear nowadays when parents, on the occasion of their child's baptism, make a genuine rediscovery of the meaning of their own baptism. In this way, as the Church re-expresses its own mystery of faith on the occasion of some specific stage in the life of men, it effects its own transformation. Its message more fully penetrates and transforms even those who proclaim it. This is an aspect we have rather forgotten in our sacramental theology. It must be rediscovered and brought to the fore so that Christians may come to feel that they have a share in the sacramental actions which some of their number are performing.

Celebration

It may seem a novelty to assign this third function to sacramental symbolism. And, in fact, it is novel, at least at the level of terminology. For a decade now, the expressions "say Mass," "read the breviary," and "perform a baptism or marriage" have been replaced by phrases with the word "celebrate." People "celebrate" the Eucharist or a baptism or a marriage. The word "celebration" is fashionable, to the point where it is used to refer to any and every sacramental action. Thus you hear: "Were you at today's celebration?" "Are you coming to celebrate with me?"

To this first observation we may add a second which has to do with the unqualified application of the word "celebration." At first sight the term might seem to apply only to sacramental actions which have a certain solemnity and are marked by a relatively high degree of formality. And yet in fact the term designates a wide range of activity. Thus a pontifical Mass in a cathedral will be called a Eucharistic celebration by the same title as the daily Mass in a rural church or a Eucharist celebrated by a small group in a living room or dining room. The word is also applied to ceremonies quite different from one another in character. We speak of celebrating a funeral, where the mood is one of sorrow, as well as of celebrating a marriage, where joy and happiness are the dominant feelings.

We have, then, two observations: the word "celebration" is a novelty in liturgical terminology, and it is used to designate quite different kinds of actions. In fact, it is applied to a very great variety of ecclesial activities.

In the following pages we shall endeavor to clarify the meaning of "celebration" as used in the context of sacramental activity. First, we shall situate celebration in relation to human activity in general by showing what its basis is. Then, after having specified the concept of celebration by comparison with that of festival, we shall describe the Christian celebration by trying to determine its object, its function, and its relations with the word.

Celebration and life

Without going into a lengthy phenomenological analysis of man's social behavior, we can state that the celebration, like the festival, is part of human activity independently of any consideration of religion. The celebration and the festival do not belong specifically to the religious sphere. We celebrate anniversaries of every kind: births, marriages, national events, etc. Men institute certain festivals that the whole nation celebrates, for example, Labor Day, Thanksgiving, and others.

The festival and the celebration have their roots in the depths of man's nature and consciousness. They express two fundamental needs of man: the desire to get away periodically from the pressures of everyday life and of time in order to grasp the depth and fullness hidden in the everyday and the temporal, and the desire for a more profound communion with the social groups which define him.

The activities in which man engages limit him to a precise moment of time and confine him within the daily round. Everything contributes to this situation: the use of time, the timetable, the demands of the moment. The person who experiences this imprisonment within a segment of time and a limited social setting feels a profound need to pull free of the constraints of time and to burst the iron fetters of the everyday. He longs to escape from time and the daily routine. The festival and the celebration answer to this felt need, for they "constitute an interruption in the obligation to work, a release from the limitations and servitude of the human condition."[36]

---

36. Roger Caillois, *Man and the Sacred*, tr. Meyer Barash (Glencoe, Ill., 1959), p. 126.

Though the celebration and the festival are themselves located within time, they transport man outside of time; they transcend time, as it were, and they transcend everyday life. They do so in order that man may penetrate more deeply into the reality of time and grasp its density and fullness. A celebration is a privileged moment in which man can become aware of the real sources of his life, aware of what he is beyond the everyday routine and of what gives him meaning.

Take as an example the celebration of a twenty-fifth wedding anniversary. For the spouses it is the much-desired opportunity for bringing to the surface of consciousness the love that has sustained them in their life together during these years. It is also the occasion for them to stand back from their daily routine and from time in order to look at what is essential in their lives and to reconsider the foundations of their existence. To this end, the celebration and the festival introduce man into a world that is very different from the world of work. They transport him into a world of freedom, gratuitousness, fraternity, and sociableness.

The celebration and the festival are also the privileged expression of another of man's needs: the need to be in communion with those who make up the different social groups which define him. In daily life the individual is frequently in contact with people. These contacts, however, are usually related to service and effective action, competition and profit, and have nothing to do with equality, affection, and gratuitousness. The celebration and the festival answer the need for communion which daily life does not allow us to satisfy.

It is interesting to note that certain festivals, though celebrated by workers in a single factory, a single institution, or a single neighborhood, nonetheless make possible encounters at a quite different level. At these festivals people reveal themselves as they really are, start friendships, create solidarities. The festival becomes a time of freedom and gratuitousness, a place for affective expression. It is thus a time for coming together, a time that allows the individual to communicate with the group and establish relationships of great personal value to him. This is important because the individual needs the groups that define him as a social being.

It is the function of the festival and the celebration to satisfy the need of communion between individuals and the group. They thus develop man as a social entity and integrate him more fully into the body to which he belongs. The reason for their existence is to enable those people to share their lives whom time and the tasks of daily life normally keep apart. They prove indispensable to man, for human life involves more than social and political structures. The fulfillment of our human and therefore our Christian vocation calls for something more. This is why we feel the need for moments of festivity and celebration at regular intervals. Father Traets asserts that "we must not fail to cultivate an awareness of the sources of meaning which these moments of festival provide for the clarification and fulfillment of our existence, a clarification and fulfillment that are less the result of our own efforts and analyses than they are a gift that is offered to us."[37]

Now that the foundation of our discussion has been laid, it is time to distinguish between celebration and festival. Both indeed answer profound human needs: the desire to escape from the dull daily round, and the desire to achieve a level of social communion. To this extent, celebration and festival are closely connected. Each calls for the other: the festival issues in the celebration, and the celebration has the festival for its basis. The celebration is in a sense the high point of the festival, the moment when the festival attains its most intense expression of community.

We must point out, however, that there can be a celebration that is not festive in its nature and mode of expression. This is the case with funerals and certain national events that are attended by sorrow. Man can therefore celebrate without holding festival. He can celebrate an anniversary, an event, a presence, in extreme solitude or in very close intimacy. Even in these circumstances the celebration provides him with an opportunity to recover in depth his own identity and to give new vitality to his existence. A celebration may thus be of a more interior character than a festival.

A festival, on the other hand, supposes a certain degree of solemnity. It is a season or time set apart. As such, it comprises various activities, some usual, others exceptional. Among these activities the celebration has a unique place because it specifies the festival, expresses it, and is its moment of greatest intensity. The celebration is a communal action that signifies and makes real the assent of the participants to the object of the festival, be this an event or a material thing. The object is never the festival for its own sake, but rather for the sake of what it represents in the lives of the participants. Here is where symbolism comes in, for

---

37. "Orientations pour une théologie des sacrements," p. 104.

the celebration becomes the locus for the unfolding of symbols. What remains to be said now of the Christian celebration as such? What is its specific character in relation to the celebration as we have been discussing it in general terms? To begin with, we must bear in mind that the Christian celebration has the same bases as any other celebration, secular or religious. At the same time, however, it is distinguished from these others by a number of factors which we shall now indicate.

First of all, the Christian celebration is to be distinguished from cultus or worship. Admittedly, the Christian liturgy has been taken as cultus in a limited sense of this term, and this usage is now traditional. We must note, however, that the New Testament represents a break with both Jewish and pagan cultus, and does not even use the "cultus." As we know, the same is true of the concept and term "priest."[38]

In the Jewish and pagan worlds, the concept of cultus or worship had resonances which were alien to the Christian definition of worship. Cultus usually implied an idolatrous worship or idolatrous devotions, a sacralization of persons and objects, reverential attitudes based on fear, a superstitious outlook or practices bordering on magic, a fatalistic conception of man's destiny. There is nothing of this in Christian worship, despite similarities of garb or mythic terminology.

The notion of cultus or worship as used by the Church in its official documents can lead to misunderstandings. Many of our ordinary Christians do not, in fact, get beyond a pagan conception that derives from a natural religiosity. They see in worship simply an act by which the individuals or community seek to lift themselves toward God in order to pay him homage and acknowledge their dependence on him.[39] This is the great danger of worship, that it runs the risk of expressing no more than a natural religious feeling which has nothing specifically Christian about it. The pagans do as much! All religions share a desire to be united to the godhead. In this context, then, worship is something one gives to God. Consequently it evokes the ideas of duty, debt, and obligation; it is what we may call the worship proper to natural religion, to all pagan religion.

Worship based on faith or, better, worship that takes the form

---

38. See A. Lemaire, "Les ministères dans la recherche néo-testamentaire," *La Maison-Dieu*, no. 115 (1973), p. 32.

39. See L. Maldonado, *Vers une liturgie sécularisée* (Paris, 1971), p. 17.

of the celebration of the mysteries of the Christian faith is something quite different. To celebrate does not mean to offer worship to God or to Jesus, but to welcome the risen Lord and to commemorate with festive joy the coming of his salvation in the life of blessedness.[40] We must therefore keep consciously in mind the fact that "the direction of a celebration, unlike that of cultus, is not from us to God; it is from God to us, because to celebrate is to encounter with a welcoming spirit him whom God sends us, the risen Lord."[41]

We may now turn to the specific object of a sacramental celebration. First of all, we celebrate a person: God, Christ, the Virgin Mary, and so on. The celebration also implies the special action or significance of this person: God's action in the world and in man; the significance of Christ and the Virgin Mary in man's vocation. But a celebration looks not only to this presence or action of a person; it also embraces the life of man—his past, his present, his future. There are difficulties with this idea, of course, since no one can return to the past, the present is difficult to identify, and we can only imagine the future. To solve this difficulty, celebrations make use of symbols, and one role of these symbols is precisely to render visible and present what is beyond the reach of the senses in past, present, and future reality. This is why man has recourse to symbolic rites which bring to the surface of his awareness a whole train of sentiments and perceptions from which daily life distracts him. Another function of these rites is to codify the needs which provide the basis for the festival and the celebration.

In short, what we celebrate about man is his life, not in and for itself but insofar as it is open to the presence of Christ and insofar as it is the locus of the marvelous deeds of God who is present in it. To sum up: What we hold festival for is both man's life and God himself. It follows that the object of a celebration is not a thing, such as a church or a relic; nor an idea, even a theological one such as the incarnation and redemption; nor a theme, such as friendship, love, or reconciliation; nor even a saint. No, it is always the living God who intervenes in man's history in order to enter into a covenant with him.

Let us anticipate the danger which will become more pressing as we emphasize the connection between the sacraments and life. If the sacramental celebration is to be different from other cele-

---

40. See C. Duchesneau, La célébration dans la vie chrétienne (Paris, 1975), p. 90.
41. Ibid.

brations, then it must not be allowed to celebrate only man's life. Rather, the celebration of a sacrament looks to God as active in man's life. It presupposes life, but life as revealed by the message of Christ. In sum, what we celebrate is God acting in our lives. Moreover, if we celebrate, it is not solely to offer him worship, to render him homage through reverential worship, but it is in order to be one in him "as the Father is in the Son and the Son in the Father."[42]

The goal of the celebration, then, is the covenant of God with man and the communion of men among themselves. Everything— the word, the songs, the prayers, the rites, the gestures—is geared to bring about this twofold communion of men among themselves and of men with God. All the elements in the celebration, by reason of their symbolic value, are means of bringing about and manifesting the invisible communion of men with one another and with God. The celebration is thus a charged time which already effects a certain communion while also providing an image of an even greater communion to which man is invited.

This understanding of Christian celebration enables us to see once again the importance of the word of God. It is possible, of course, to celebrate life without the aid of the message that is contained in the word. It is not possible, however, without the help of the revelatory word, to celebrate life insofar as it manifests the great deeds of God on behalf of men. This statement speaks of what, in classical sacramental theology, would be called matter and form, but it helps us remove the restrictive elements in the notions of matter and form.

The intention of the classical thesis on matter and form in sacramental theology was to define a sacrament as a composite of two elements, one of them visible, namely, the "thing" used, and the other invisible but expressed by the word, the *verbum*. St. Thomas has recourse to the philosophical theory known as hylomorphism, which he uses, however, with many cautions and nuances. Thus he says repeatedly that a sacrament is composed of two elements which are related "like matter and form." For example: "And thus in the sacraments words and things form a kind of unity, comparable to that resulting from form and matter."[43] Or: "In the sacraments words function after the fashion of a form, while sensible things function after the fashion of matter."[44]

---

42. Jn. 17:21.
43. *Summa theologiae* III, q. 60, a. 6, ad 2.
44. *Ibid.*, III, q. 60, a. 7c.

Unfortunately, later Scholasticism was more faithful to the letter of St. Thomas than to his spirit, and turned his position here into a straight philosophical and technical doctrine of the sacraments in which no account was taken of the role of the word that is received in faith. And yet for St. Augustine and St. Thomas, in the very nature of things it is this word of faith which sheds light on man's concrete life that must be given a place in the sacraments. It must be admitted that one effect of the development of canon law from the tenth century on was to remove the sap from this thesis on matter and form and to cause its rich underlying intuition to be forgotten.

As we have presented it, the Christian celebration embraces both human life and the presence of the risen Lord who sheds his light on that life. As a result, however, of the juridical application of the thesis on matter and form, Christians have ended up understanding only an infinitesimal part of either human life or the word as these enter the sacramental celebration. We must therefore break away from the restrictive concepts of matter and form if we are to see that the whole of life (even if under a particular aspect) and the whole mystery of the risen Lord are the object of the sacramental celebration.

As a matter of fact, this way of expressing the point is not so very different from the Scholastic approach to matter and form in sacramental theology. For the Scholastics were careful to say that there is both a proximate matter and form and a remote matter and form in the sacraments. The remote matter and form, however, were increasingly ignored, and for practical purposes only the proximate matter and form were retained. This phenomenon can be explained by the law of the minimum which prevailed in Christian sacramentality, as well as by the juridical preoccupation with guaranteeing validity and liceity. In fact, however, the basic intuition of the Scholastics embraced the whole of life and the entire mystery of the risen Lord.

This, then, is a dimension that needs to be rediscovered and emphasized. Thus, for example, the object of the Christian celebration of marriage is the entire love-filled life of man and woman, and not simply the moment at which they exchange their consents. So too, what clarifies and illumines human life is the entire mystery of the risen Lord and not simply the formula by which consent is mutually given for marriage or the formula of sacramental absolution or the formula of Christian baptism.

A Christian celebration calls for the service of the entire assembly, for the latter is the subject that celebrates. It is the community that gathers, prays, sings, proclaims, attests, and bears witness. It takes priority over any and every gesture, rite, prayer, formula, etc., and it gives meaning to all these. The first Christians were aware of the primacy of the assembly. They used to gather almost anywhere. Because they had none of the appurtenances—churches, objects used in liturgy, liturgical vestments—they focused on the essential and nothing but the essential. Their liturgy was simply the gathering for celebration of those who believed in Jesus Christ. Thus conceived, the assembly became the clearest manifestation of the priestly status of all the participants. The celebration became the exercise of the priesthood of the faithful.

This is a point of doctrine which Vatican II has endeavored to bring out in its liturgical renewal, and it entails many consequences both for the lay participants and for the ordained minister. Inasmuch as they form the celebrating assembly which is an actant in the celebration, the faithful are being induced to take an increasingly active role and themselves to become actants in the celebration. This is happening to such a degree that people sometimes ask what is left of the priest's specific role. And indeed the priest's role as ordained minister is changing. He is no longer the only one active in the celebration. His mission is to preside over the celebrating assembly, not to take its place. His presidency has to do with the communion of those gathered, and this in two ways. First, at the local level, he is to help bring about the communion of Christians among themselves and with the risen Lord. But he is also to help bring about the communion of this assembly with other Christian assemblies. He becomes responsible for that communion which is the purpose of the Christian celebration.

Here is the place for some remarks on the assembly and the community. For some time now in the Church, there has been a good deal of emphasis on the community. Some persons deplore the absence of genuine Christian communities; others devote all their energies to building real Christian communities. It is essential, however, to make some distinctions when we speak about "communion," "assembly," and "community." According to the ecclesiology of *Lumen gentium*, the important thing is to establish communion: communion of men among themselves, and communion of men with the Father, the Son, and the Spirit. In the attainment of this objective, the New Testament lays a good deal of stress on the assembly, to the point that the Greek word *ekklesia,* which means "assembly," became the regular name for the whole group of Christians.

Currently, a great deal of emphasis is being placed on the very noble objective for forming communities, but we may ask just what people have in mind as they attempt to bring this about. Do they not always have in the back of their minds as a model the familiar rural community which was the sum total of all activities? There the parish was the locus of worship, life, trade, leisure, etc. But, given the fact that people today belong simultaneously to various kinds of groups, what kind of Christian community should we be endeavoring to build? It seems to us that goal is a vague one, since divergent understandings of the idea of community are abroad. Should we not seek to clarify what we mean by community by taking into account the desires and needs of men as well as the contemporary sociological context?

In some places the idea of Christian community had acquired its own special tonality, and the community had taken on certain functions according to the sociological context of the time. Now that all that has changed, it is time to rethink the Christian community in terms both of its functions and of its sociological contours. Should we not be working to form assemblies out of which various types of community might arise? The idea of assembly or gathering seems more functional, less institutionalized. It is a means, not an end. We do not gather for the sake of gathering but in order to pray, celebrate, keep festival, share a sorrow, a joy, an endeavor, collaborate in a common project, and so on. The assembly is at the service of fraternal communion and fraternal love.

This last point is all the more important, since our ecclesial assemblies often lack motivation. There is reason therefore to develop such motivation, and to this end the best means seems to be an effort to create bonds of all kinds. With this kind of communion as their goal, assemblies should stimulate in the participants a sense of belonging and, in consequence, a need to participate in the life of the community, a life that extends far beyond the place of assembly. In view of the crisis that is agitating all communities, secular as well as Christian, we might, with communion as our goal, work to establish various kinds of gatherings that would produce a type of community which will inevitably be less all-embracing than the type we have previously known.

As the third function of sacramental activity, the celebration is not isolated from the components of the sacramental order. It is very closely bound up with the Church and man who take part in the sacramental action, just as it has extensive connections with the other two functions of proclamation and actualization. Celebration is a form of proclamation. We need to correct here a Christian outlook that identified, and still identifies, the sacrament with the celebration of the rite as such, and saw in the proclamation of the message only a preparation for the real sacrament. This outlook is the fruit of a juridical emphasis, an individualistic approach, and a "pinpointing" conception of the sacraments. Once that outlook is corrected, we must look at sacramental activity in its totality, while admitting, however, that it has various stages which are divided by more important moments that intensify and render perceptible a new awareness, a communion, and a real transformation.

Nor is celebration independent of actualization, for it is precisely a locus of realization or actualization; it represents a new consciousness; it is an invitation to a real transformation.

Finally, the celebration is closely linked with the three dimensions of sacramental activity of which we shall speak immediately after finishing these thoughts on the functions of a sacrament. The object of the celebration is not a state of life as such nor the God once revealed by Jesus. Rather, the object is the God who has revealed himself, is revealing himself, and will reveal himself, and a dimension of man's life that has already become real, is becoming real today in a concrete and visible way, and is called to become more perfectly real in the eschatological time which we await. In summary, the celebration becomes a moment and a place where a whole past and a whole present take on a new meaning. It recapitulates all previous experience and turns man toward the future.

Conclusion

We have distinguished the three functions of sacramental symbolism. This was necessary if we were to better analyze and identify a reality that is quite complex. The sacramental activity of Christ, the Church, and man proclaims, actualizes, and celebrates the presence and action of God in human life. We have already pointed out that the three functions overlap as it were, to the point where it is difficult at times to know what belongs to a given function. We are not dealing with three functions superimposed one upon the other like three stories of a house; because of its power of evocation, sacramental symbolic activity can exercise the three functions simultaneously. Thus the word proclaimed and sung can have the function of proclaiming, actualizing, and celebrating.

It should be noted, furthermore, that each sacramental action does not highlight in the same way the various functions and actants or the various dimensions of which we shall be speaking in a moment. The new ritual of penance takes this fact into account. It is clear that in the private celebration of penance the role of the community is somewhat eclipsed and that the emphasis is on the step being taken by the individual. The rite of communal penance, on the other hand, stresses the place of the Church. It is the same with the other sacramental actions: some emphasize the function of proclamation, while others emphasize rather the function of celebration. It is important to keep this kind of variety in mind, since it is impossible in practice to experience simultaneously and in the same degree all the functions and dimensions of the sacraments, just as it is impossible to involve Christ, the Church, and the individual in the same way and to the same degree. This is why we must elaborate various kinds of sacramental services.

Just as the Church became aware that it had to take advantage of a number of human situations in order to fulfill its own vocation as a sacrament, so too, it needs a number of types of celebration for baptism, marriage, etc., if it is to make explicit all the functions and dimensions of one and the same sacrament. Thus one celebration of the Eucharist can truly bring out the communion already existing among Christians, while another can emphasize the communion still to be achieved. Given all the riches that are to be exploited, we must accept the fact that we cannot bring them all out at the same time, for if we tried to, we would end up proclaiming nothing, actualizing nothing, and celebrating nothing. It is better to emphasize one or other function or dimension while counting on the possibility of producing other types of celebration that will emphasize other aspects.

4 — The Dimensions of Sacramental Symbolism

To complete our understanding of the Christian sacraments, we must point to another aspect which, in dependence on the classical formulation, we shall call the three dimensions of the sacramental sign. Under this heading we shall be making our own a doctrine that is part of the central biblical, patristic, and Scholastic tradition. Despite its prestige, however, this doctrine has not been given its due place in contemporary thinking on the sacraments. It would take too long to survey the biblical, patristic, and Scholastic evidence on the question. However, we shall present a bit of it as we go into each of the dimensions. Our point of departure will be an article of St. Thomas.

In his discussion of the sacraments and signification, St. Thomas asks whether a sacrament is the sign of a single reality. His answer is very illuminating. For him a sacrament is the sign of a threefold reality. It is a commemorative sign of a past reality, a demonstrative (in the literal sense of "pointing to") sign of a present reality, and a prefigurative sign of a reality yet to come.[45] In this thesis St. Thomas shows us the three dimensions of every sacramental action and sums up the teaching of Christian tradition down to his day.

In these theological reflections St. Thomas is presenting in his own manner the biblical conception of Jewish worship and of the Christian celebration. When the Jews celebrated the Passover, they were recalling the crossing of the Red Sea, and thus the liberation of Israel from slavery in Egypt. By commemorating this historical event, they were making it present to themselves; they were conscious that the past event had serious implications for their present lives. Finally, Jewish worship proclaimed, by prefiguring it, a saving event, another but definitive liberation which had at a certain point in the religious history of Israel acquired the name of "the Day of Yahweh." Thus the Jewish Passover meal not only commemorated the liberation of Israel and brought its effects into focus for each generation; it also proclaimed and prefigured another kind of liberation that would be even more definitive and complete: the liberation which the Messiah was to effect.[46]

This whole concept was largely taken over and utilized by St. Paul, the Fathers of the Church, and the medieval theologians, to say nothing of the liturgical texts themselves. As we discuss each dimension in detail, we shall see more clearly the significance of this thesis in sacramental theology and its impact on the celebration of the sacraments.

---

45. *Summa theologiae* III, q. 60, a. 3c; J.-M. Tillard, O.P., has provided a lengthy commentary on this article in his essay "La triple dimension du signe sacramental (à propos de *Sum. Theol.* III, 60, 3)," *Nouvelle revue théologique* 83 (1961), pp. 225–54.

46. This whole view of the Passover meal is treated under the rubric of "memorial." On the subject see Max Thurian, *The Eucharistic Memorial*, tr. J. G. Davies (Ecumenical Studies in Worship 7–8; Richmond, Va., 1961), Vol. 1, *passim*; Bas van Iersel, "Some Biblical Roots of the Christian Sacrament," pp. 6–15.

The commemorative sign

When St. Thomas speaks of a sacrament as a commemorative sign, he is referring to that which is the cause of our salvation, the passion of Christ. The sacrament is a representation of a past event. This aspect of a sacrament has a long history behind it. As we noted, it was present in Jewish worship, in what is called the memorial. The Jews who celebrated the Passover recalled or commemorated the crossing of the Red Sea and the liberation of Israel from slavery in Egypt. The first Christians adopted this model for their own celebration, especially their celebration of the Eucharistic mystery. The Christian assembly commemorated the mystery of Jesus and its own entry into that mystery.

A number of patristic writings as well as the liturgy itself show how well this scheme fitted the Eucharist. In fact, it was developed and given pride of place in all thinking about the Eucharist. But we must bear in mind that it applied as well to all the other sacraments. Baptism, for example, recalls the death and resurrection of Christ.[47] Confirmation refers back to what Jesus says about the gift of the Spirit and to the experience of this gift which the apostles had after the death of Jesus. And so on. We must not think, however, that the recall is limited solely to the mystery of Christ; it refers to this, certainly, but it also refers to the many prefigurations of that mystery and to its many actualizations in the life of Christians. Thus penance refers to the central mystery of reconciliation, which is the paschal mystery, but it also commemorates the many reconciliations which Yahweh had effected between his people and himself and to the countless reconciliations which Christ has brought about in the lives of men generally and of Christians in particular since the days when he was on this earth.

It is already a great deal that the sacraments should signify this past to the Christian of today. But to say only this much is to run the risk of making a sacrament simply a way of remembering the past; the wealth of sacramental symbolism would be reduced to a minimum. For, in addition to being a commemorative sign, the sacramental symbol is a demonstrative sign of a present reality.

The demonstrative sign[48]

A sacrament does not signify only the past, important though

---

47. Rom. 6:3.

48. We have decided to keep the terminology of St. Thomas, since we think it affords no difficulty as far as the commemorative and prefigurative aspects are concerned. The term "demonstrative," on the other hand, can be a difficulty; it may appear to be rather technical. We shall keep it, nonetheless, since we think the explanation to be given will help the reader to understand it properly.

the past is. Its purpose is also to render perceptible and make manifest what this past has left as a heritage for the present life of the Christian. This dimension too, we may recall, was present in Old Testament worship. It calls to mind the saving acts of God in terms of their value for the present life and of the consequences they ought to have as far as man's behavior is concerned. It is a matter of signifying the implications of one or other aspect of the mystery of Christ for the today of the individual or community. The liturgical expression "today" can help us clarify this dimension of the sacramental symbol. The word refers to the permanent and ongoing presence of Christ in man's life, but in relation to a particular mystery, as for example the incarnation. The "today" signifies Christ's presence in man in every generation.

This "today" applies to each of the sacraments. For the Eucharist the matter is perfectly clear. A number of authors have taken this approach in commenting on the words "Do this in remembrance of me."[49] St. Paul himself had already made an important addition to the account of the Last Supper when he said in 1 Cor. 11:26: "For as often as you eat this bread and drink this cup, you proclaim the Lord's death until he comes." The whole of St. Paul's theology of the Lord's Supper implies among other things that the celebration of the memorial is more than a representation of the Supper; it is an actualization of the death of Jesus on the cross. What it calls to mind is indeed the death of the Lord, that is, the saving and redemptive action of God in the Lord Jesus, but it recalls it as an action in which all the guests at the meal participate by the act of celebrating it.

Even though this dimension is more obvious in the Lord's Supper, it is present in every sacrament. In baptism, penance, confirmation, the anointing of the sick, etc., we do not simply recall a past; we actualize the paschal mystery in the today of the community and of each believer. To celebrate a sacrament, then, is not simply to revive the memory of the cross and Easter; it is to relive these saving events today, to gather the fruit of them, to profit by their dynamism. In other words, the saving act of Christ is always actual and everywhere present, even though it remains hidden from the person who does not have faith. The main role of the sacramental action is to render that act present to the entire everyday life of man, but in particular to the special moments

---

49. See, for example, Max Thurian, *The Eucharistic Memorial*, Vol. 2; J. de Baciocchi and H. Verder, *Eucharistie* (Paris, 1975).

of his existence, such as his birth, his growth, his death, and so on. In saying that the sacrament is a demonstrative sign of a present reality, we mean that the sacrament actualizes the paschal mystery and renders it present in man's life. Its function is to show him the implications of this mystery and make him become conscious of its actuality.

The prefigurative sign

To the two foregoing dimensions St. Thomas adds a third: the sign is prefigurative. Like the other two, this dimension has roots in Old Testament worship. When the Jews celebrated the liberation of Israel, they were commemorating the event and reliving it as related to them, but they were also proclaiming, by way of a prefiguration, another and definitive saving event. This dimension, like the other two, has had a profound influence on the texts of the Christian liturgy. Thus the prayers of the Eucharistic liturgy are often constructed according to the scheme of the three dimensions. A text will make a past event, such as the death of Jesus, the basis for underscoring his presence in the contemporary world and will end by referring to a more definitive coming. The following text from the Midnight Mass of Christmas is very typical of this format: "Lord, you made this holy night resplendent with the brilliance of the true light. Grant that, being enlightened here below by the revelation of this mystery, we may taste its joy to the full in heaven: Through Jesus Christ. . . ."

The entire liturgy transports us into this future world as it speaks of heaven and all that goes with it. It is important to emphasize that this dimension used to be a part of the Christian outlook at one time. Today it seems to have been neglected in order to concentrate in a more concrete way on the present and thus to bring the liturgy closer to life. The difficulty seems in fact to be a matter of language. People feel ill at ease with the classical categories of Christian theology and the Christian liturgy as a means of presenting the eschatological dimension of Christian existence. The need, therefore, is to formulate a new language for presenting and making vividly real this dimension of eschatological expectation.

We undoubtedly know, and say in our songs, that the Lord will come and establish his definitive Kingdom. But do we draw the conclusions that are implicit in this belief? Are they sufficiently clear in our celebrations to give a direction and stimulus to Christian life? In point of fact, all of Christian existence should be turned prophetically toward this future. Christians should be in the front ranks of those who proclaim the Kingdom and build the world so that it may be a truly habitable place and a sign of the new earth. From this point of view, sacramental celebrations are a stimulus to push ahead to the world that is to come, because they proclaim to man the possibility of entering this new earth. They inspire hope despite seeming obstacles. Like Christian life itself, there can be no celebration that is not oriented to the future and does not revive hope.

In the concrete, this means that a sacramental action should always keep this eschatological dimension in view. In the case of the Eucharist, for example, the celebration gives a conspicuous place to the communion that is symbolized by the meal. It renders visible the communion of Christ with men and with his Father, and it proclaims the possibility of a still more profound communion of men with one another and with the Father, the Son, and the Spirit. It proclaims this possibility despite the obstacles that may seem to defeat its realization. The sacrament gives the Christian a hope against all hope and draws him into its own dynamic movement.

The pattern is just as clear in the celebration of reconciliation as it is in the Eucharist. This sacrament is a sign revealing the great reconciliation which Christ effected between mankind and his Father; it is a demonstrative sign of a reconciliation here and now of the community with God and of the members with one another; but it is also the prefigurative sign of a perfect reconciliation that is to come.

It goes without saying that these three dimensions of a sacrament are interwoven with its functions of revelation, actualization, and celebration. At the pastoral level the recognition of this fact is important for bringing out the real significance of the Christian mystery and locating the Christian within a dynamic movement that has no end. Thus the proclamation which is effected by the liturgy and by the entire sacramental process that accompanies it and gives it its basis must keep these three dimensions clearly in view. How minimizing and limited in outlook is a pastoral approach to the sacraments that insists only on the first two dimensions and lets the Christian believe that the process is now terminated, whereas in reality a sacrament introduces the Christian into a process that is unending!

In conclusion, we must bear in mind that a sacrament reveals three aspects or dimensions of the mystery of God and therefore of the mystery of man as well. In referring us to the eschatological future, the sacrament sketches an image of that future for us now, and the image in turn imposes a duty on us: that we bear witness to what the sacrament is saying. From one point of view, a sacrament bodies forth a utopia that has its basis in the risen Christ and represents man's fulfillment. A sacrament, says Moltmann, is always running ahead of itself and of our experience. It thereby brings a dynamism into play, creates a hope, and sets man on the road to his realization and fulfillment.

At the same time, the sacrament causes the assembly to feel the pain of not yet being, in its witness and its daily life, what the sacrament commands it to be. For a sacrament often signifies not what the Church and man now are, but rather what they ought to be. By that very fact, a sacrament functions as a critique of our lives as Christians. The sacramental rites act as critic even of the Church itself and confront it with the image of what it ought to be. The Church will never in fact be what the Eucharist calls upon it to be. The sacrament always runs ahead of the Church and man. Such is the dynamism proper to it.

Conclusion

The constitutive elements of the sacraments, as these were explained in the final chapter, may seem to be rather scattered. That is often the impression left by an analysis. And yet the elements form a whole. By way of conclusion, we shall go back over these various elements and try to get a better view of their internal articulation and coherence. We shall give these final pages the form of a descriptive theological definition.

A Christian sacrament can be regarded as the symbolic activity of the Church, of Christ, and of man. It is in a sense the most eloquent sign of the Church, of Christ, and of man. The sign in this instance is not a mere signal, but a symbolic sign in the richest sense of the term, as explained above all by Karl Rahner.[1]

By reason of its symbolic value, the sacramental activity of the Church, Christ, and man reveals the mystery of God and the meaning of man's own life. It actualizes this mystery and meaning, and celebrates them, so that sacramental activity or the sacraments become the sign of a Church that in the name of Christ Jesus manifests to mankind the true face of both God and man. And not only their face here and now, but the past of God and man, and what they will become in relation to one another. The sacraments are the sign of a Church that re-expresses its own mystery and attends to the implications of the mystery of God and of the true face of man as revealed by the risen Lord.

This revelation of God and man is not addressed solely to the mind. It is meant to be concrete, dynamic, and transformative.

---

1. "The Theology of the Symbol."

The sacraments thus take flesh in man's life; they take root in him and transform him. This power is inherent in the word of revelation, which becomes a creative word, so that the sacraments become the sign of a Church that, acting always in the name of Christ, actualizes the message of Jesus in its own life. The revelation of a God who is himself a communion, and the revelation of man as called to imitate this communion, rouse and incite men to a real communion among themselves. Finally, the sacraments are the sign of a Church that celebrates the revelation of a new face of God, the possibility of man becoming new, and that same newness as already begun.

The sacraments also signify the action of Christ, who, through the Church, reveals to the world the face of both God and man, makes both of these real in himself to an eminent degree, and celebrates them in joy and peace. Even more than the Church, Christ Jesus reveals all this in all three of its dimensions. That is to say, he reveals, actualizes, and celebrates the true being of God and man by commemorating his own mystery, fulfilling it, and prefiguring the future.

Finally, the sacraments are a privileged occasion for man—be he a believer who is already part of the Church or a nonbeliever—to become aware of God's identity, of his own identity, and of the goal to which he is moving. Man discovers these values at privileged moments of his own life and the lives of others. In this way the sacraments become the sign of man who discovers the true face of God and at the same time his own true face. He becomes attentive to the implications of his discovery, the requirements it imposes, and the stimulus it contains. He reproduces these faces in his life and, with the Christian assembly that is gathered in the name of Christ, he celebrates this entire universe of God and man that transcends him.

Christian sacramentality has thus to do with visibility, at the level both of being and of action. This visibility includes the entire being and activity of Jesus, who is acknowledged as Christ and Lord, the entire being and activity of the Church, which is the community of believers, and the entire being and activity of the man who is moved by the Spirit. The sacraments are thus the expression of Christ, the Church, and man, both in their being and in their activity. They express the depths of the being of all three, and at the same time they are the means by which the three—Christ, the Church, and man—express themselves.

122

Conclusion

We can present this descriptive theological definition schematically as follows:

The sacramental activity
of the Church
or
the sacraments
are the sign

$\left\{\vphantom{\begin{array}{c}a\\a\\a\\a\end{array}}\right.$

of a Church which
—*reveals* the face of God and the face of man
—*actualizes* (incarnates) these faces (by proclaiming them in a prefigurative way)
—*celebrates* this revelation, the here-and-now actualization of this revelation, and the hope of its definitive actualization

of Christ who, through his Church,
—*reveals* the face of God and the face of man in its perfect form
—*makes real* and visible what God is and what man is
—*celebrates* the mystery of God and the mystery of man

of man who
—*discovers* who God is and what he himself is (what he is now and what he is called to become)
—*allows* himself to be transformed and transforms himself in accordance with the vision of God and with the eschatological image of himself as revealed in Jesus
—*celebrates* this mystery of God and man in union with the assembly of Christians

Bibliography

Anciaux, P. *Sacrement et vie*. Tournai: Casterman, 1967.

Coffy, R., and Varro, R. *Église, signe du salut au milieu des hommes*. Paris: Le Centurion, 1972.

Coffy, R., Valadier, P., and Streiff, J. *Une Église qui célèbre et qui prie*. Paris: Le Centurion, 1974.

Congar, Y. *Un peuple messianique*. Cogitatio fidei 85. Paris: Le Cerf, 1975.

Denis, H. *Des sacrements et des hommes*. Paris: Le Chalet, 1975.

————, "Les sacrements ont-ils un avenir?" in Lex orandi 52. Paris: Le Cerf, 1971.

De Jong, J. P. *L'Eucharistie comme réalité symbolique*. Cogitatio fidei 65. Paris: Le Cerf, 1972.

Didier, R. *Les sacrements de la foi*. Paris: Le Centurion, 1975.

Duchesnau, Cl. *La célébration dans la vie chrétienne*. Paris: Le Centurion, 1975.

Grand'maison, J. *Symboliques d'hier et d'aujourd'hui*. Montreal: Hurtubise, 1974.

Moingt, J. *Le devenir chrétien*. Paris: Desclée De Brouwer, 1973.

Monfort, F. *Les sacrements, pour quoi faire?* Paris: Le Cerf, 1975.

Pannikar, R. *Worship and Secular Man*. Maryknoll: Orbis, 1973.

Rahner, K. *The Church and the Sacraments*, translated by W. J.

O'Hara. *Quaestiones Disputatae* 9. New York: Herder and Herder, 1963.

_____, "The Theology of the Symbol," in his *Theological Investigations* 4, translated by K. Smyth. Baltimore: Helicon, 1966, pp. 221-52.

Ratzinger, J. *Un seul Seigneur, une seule foi.* Paris: Mame, 1971.

Robinson, J.A.T. *The Difference in Being a Christian Today.* Philadelphia: Westminster, 1972.

Rondet, H. *La vie sacramentaire.* Paris: Fayard, 1972.

Schillebeeckx, E. *Christ the Sacrament of the Encounter with God,* translated by P. Barrett. New York: Sheed & Ward, 1963.

Tillard, J.M.R. *Le sacrement événement de salut.* Études religieuses 765. Brussels: La Pensée Catholique, 1964.

Traets, C. "Orientations pour une théologie des sacrements," *Questions liturgiques* 53 (1972), pp. 97–118.

Vaillancourt, R. "Du rite sacramentel à la sacramentalité de l'Église," *Cahiers de Pastorale Scolaire,* no. 6. Sherbrooke: Faculté de théologie, Université de Sherbrooke, 1976.

_____et al. *L'Eucharistie, le sens des sacrements.* Lyons: Faculté de théologie de Lyon, 1971.

_____ et al. *Les sacrements d'initiation et les ministères sacrés.* Paris: Fayard, 1974.

Concilium, no. 31: "The Sacraments in General."

La Maison-Dieu, no. 119: "Anthropologie sacramentelle."